D0544568

THE THIRTEENTH CANDLE

is T. Lobsang Rampa's thirteenth book.
It answers many questions which Dr.
Rampa is often asked about the world of
the astral, healing, life after death, and
similar topics. Like his earlier books,
THE THIRTEENTH CANDLE will bring
consolation and inspiration to countless
readers—in particular, to Dr. Rampa's
many students and followers.

Also by T. Lobsang Rampa

TWILIGHT
CANDLELIGHT
THE HERMIT
FEEDING THE FLAME
LIVING WITH THE LAMA
BEYOND THE TENTH
CHAPTERS OF LIFE
YOU — FOREVER
THE SAFFRON ROBE
THE RAMPA STORY
WISDOM OF THE ANCIENTS
DOCTOR FROM LHASA
THE THIRD EYE
THE CAVE OF THE ANCIENTS
AS IT WAS!
I BELIEVE
THREE LIVES

and published by CORGI BOOKS

T. Lobsang Rampa

The Thirteenth Candle

CORGI BOOKS
A DIVISION OF TRANSWORLD PUBLISHERS LTD

₦2.50

THE THIRTEENTH CANDLE

A CORGI BOOK o 552 08880 3

First publication in Great Britain

PRINTING HISTORY
Corgi edition published 1972
Corgi edition reprinted 1972
Corgi edition reprinted 1973 (twice)
Corgi edition reprinted 1974
Corgi edition reprinted 1976
Corgi edition reprinted 1977
Corgi edition reprinted 1979
Corgi edition reprinted 1980

The extract from the *Montreal Star* on pages 10–11 is
reprinted by permission of The Canadian Press

This book is set in Pilgrim 10 pt

Corgi Books are published by Transworld Publishers Ltd,
Century House, 61–63 Uxbridge Road,
Ealing, London W5 5SA.
Made and printed in Great Britain by
Hunt Barnard Printing Ltd, Aylesbury, Bucks.

EXPLANATION

'The Thirteenth Candle?' Well, it is meant to be a logical title derived from what I am trying to do. I am trying to 'light a candle' which is far better than 'cursing the darkness'. This is my thirteenth book which, I hope, will be my Thirteenth Candle.

You may think it is a very little candle, perhaps one of those birthday-cake candles. But I have never had a cake of any kind with candles—never even had a birthday cake! —and now with my restricted sugar-free, low-residue diet of not more than a thousand calories it is too late to bother.

So indulge me; let's pretend that this is 'The Thirteenth Candle' even though it be as small as the candle on a doll's birthday cake.

CHAPTER ONE

Mrs. Martha MacGoohoogly strode purposefully to her kitchen door, a tattered scrap of newspaper clutched in a ham-like hand. Outside, in the parched patch of weed-covered ground which served as 'back garden' she stopped and glared around like a cross bull in the mating season awaiting the advent of rivals. Satisfied—or disappointed—that there were no rivals for attention in the offing, she hurried to the broken-down fence defining the garden limits.

Gratefully propping her more than ample bosom on a worm-eaten post, she shut her eyes and opened her mouth. 'Hey, Maud!' she roared across the adjoining gardens, her voice echoing and reverberating from the nearby factory wall. 'Hey, Maud, where are ya?' Closing her mouth and opening her eyes she stood awaiting the results.

From the direction of the next-house-but-one came the sound of a plate dropping and smashing, and then the kitchen door of THAT house opened and a small, scraggy woman came hopping out, agitatedly wiping her hands on her ragged apron. 'Well?' she growled dourly. 'What d'ya want?'

'Hey, Maud, you seen this?' yelled back Martha as she waved the tattered piece of newsprint over her head.

'How do I know if I seen it if I haven't seen it first?' snorted Maud. 'I might a done, then, on the other hand, I might not. What is it, anyhow, another sex scandal?'

Mrs. Martha MacGoohoogly fumbled in the pocket of her apron and withdrew large horn-rimmed spectacles lavishly besprinkled with small stones. Carefully she wiped the glasses on the bottom of her skirt before putting them on and patting her hair in place over her ears. Then, noisily wiping her nose on the back of her sleeve, she yelled out,

'It's from the Dominion, my nephew sent it to me.'

'Dominion? What shop is that? Have they got a sale on?' called Maud with the first show of interest.

Martha snorted in rage and disgust, 'Naw!' she shouted in exasperation. 'Don't you know NUTHINK? Dominion, you know, Canada. Dominion of Canada. My nephew sent it to me. Wait a mo, I'll be right over.' Hoisting her bosom off the fence, and tucking her glasses into her apron pocket, she sped down the rough garden and into the lane at the bottom. Maud sighed with resignation and slowly went to meet her.

'Look at this!' yelled Martha as they met in the lane at the garden gate of the empty lot between their two houses. 'Look at the rot they write now. Soul? There ain't no such thing. When you're dead you're DEAD, just like that—POOF!' Her face flushed, she brandished the paper under poor Maud's long thin nose, and said angrily, 'How they get away with it I don't never know. You die, it's like blowing out a candle and with nothing after. My poor husband, God rest his soul, always said, before he died, that it would be such a relief to know that he wouldn't meet his past associates again.' She sniffed to herself at the mere thought.

Maud O'Haggis looked down the sides of her nose and waited patiently for her crony to run down. At last she seized her opportunity and asked, 'But what is this article which has so upset you?'

Speechlessly Martha MacGoohoogly passed over the tattered fragment of paper that had caused all the commotion. 'No, dear,' she suddenly said, having found her voice again. 'That's the wrong side you are reading.' Maud turned over the paper and started all over again, her lips silently forming the words as she read them. 'Well!' she exclaimed. 'Well I never!'

Martha smiled with triumphant satisfaction. 'Well,' she said. 'It's a rum do, eh, when such stuff can get into print. What d'ya make of it?'

Maud turned over the page a few times, started to read the wrong side again, and then said, 'Oh! I know, Helen Hensbaum will tell us, she knows all about these things. She reads BOOKS.'

'Aw! I can't BEAR that woman,' retorted Martha. 'Say, d'ye know what she said to me the other day? She said,

"May beets grow in your belly—God forbid, Mrs. Mac-Goohoogly." That's what she said to me, can you imagine it? The CHEEK of the woman. Pfah!'

'But she got the gen, she knows her stuff about these things, and if we want to get to the bottom of THIS'—she violently fluttered the poor unfortunate sheet of paper—'we shall have to play her game and butter her up. Come on, let's go see her.'

Martha pointed down the lane and said, 'THERE she is, hanging out her smalls, fancy hussy she is, I must say. Get a load of them new pantie hose, must be on a special somewhere. Me, good old-fashioned knickers is good enough for me.' She raised her skirt to show. 'Keeps yer warmer when there is no man about, eh?' She laughed coarsely and the two women sauntered down the lane towards Helen Hensbaum and her washing.

Just as they were about to turn into the Hensbaum garden the sound of a slamming door halted them. From the adjacent garden a Pair of the Hottest Hot Pants appeared. Fascinated, the two women stared. Slowly their gaze travelled upwards to take in the see-three blouse and vapid, painted face. 'Strewth!' muttered Maud O'Haggis. 'There's life in the old town yet!' Silently they stood and goggled as the young girl in the Hot Pants teetered by on heels as high as her morals were low.

'Makes yer feel old, like, don't it?' said Martha Mac-Goohoogly. Without another word they turned into the Hensbaum place to find Mrs. Hensbaum watching the girl going on the beat.

'The top of the morning to you, Mrs. Hensbaum,' called Martha. 'I see you have Sights at your end of the lane, eh?' She gave a throaty chuckle. Helen Hensbaum scowled even more ferociously as she looked down the lane. 'Ach! HER!' she exclaimed. 'Dead in her mother's womb she should be, already!' She sighed and stretched up to her high clothes-line, demonstrating that she DID wear pantie hose.

'Mrs. Hensbaum,' began Maud, 'we know as how you are well read and know all about such things, so we have come to you for advice.' She stopped, and Helen Hensbaum smiled as she said, 'Well now, ladies, come in, and I will make a cup of tea for you this cold morning. It'll do us all good to rest a while.' She turned and led the way into her well-kept home which had the local name of 'Little Germany' because it was so neat and tidy.

The kettle was boiling, the tea was steaming. Mrs. Hensbaum passed round sweet biscuits and then said, 'Now, what can I do for you?'

Maud gestured to Martha and said, 'She has got a queer sort of tale from Canada or some such outlandish place. Don't know what to make of it, meself. SHE'LL tell you.'

Martha sat up straighter and said, 'Here—look at this, I got it sent from my nephew. Got himself in trouble over a married woman, he did, and he scarpered off to a place called Montreal, in the Dominion. Writes sometimes. Just sent this in his letter. Don't believe in such stuff.' She passed over the tattered scrap of paper, now much the worse for rough handling.

Mrs. Helen Hensbaum gingerly took the remnant and spread it out on a clean sheet of paper. 'Ach, so!' she yelped in her excitement, quite forgetting her normally excellent English. 'Ist gut, no?'

'Will ye read it out to us, clear like, and tell us what you think?' asked Maud.

So Mrs. Hensbaum cleared her throat, sipped her tea, and started: 'From the Montreal Star, I see. Monday, May 31st, 1971. Hmmm. INTERESTING. Yes, I to that city have been.' A short pause, and she read out:

'*Saw himself leave his body. Heart Victim Describes Dying Feeling.* Canadian Press—Toronto. A Toronto man who suffered a heart attack last year, says he saw himself leave his body and had strange, tranquil sensations during a critical period when his heart stopped.

'B. Leslie Sharpe, 68, says during the period his heart was not beating he was able to observe himself "face to face".

'Mr. Sharpe describes his experience in the current issue of the Canadian Medical Association Journal in part of a report by Dr. R. L. MacMillan and Dr. K. W. G. Brown, co-directors of the coronary care unit of Toronto General Hospital.

'In the report, the doctors said, "This could be the concept of the soul leaving the body."

'Mr. Sharpe was taken to hospital after his family doctor diagnosed a pain in his left arm as a heart attack.

'The following morning, Mr. Sharpe says, he remembers

glancing at his watch while lying in bed hooked to the wires of a cardiograph machine and intravenous tubes.

' "Just then I gave a very, very deep sigh and my head flopped over to the right. I thought, 'Why did my head flop over?—I didn't move it—I must be going to sleep.'

' "Then I am looking at my own body from the waist up, face to face as though from a mirror in which I appear to be in the lower left corner. Almost immediately I saw myself leaving my body, coming out through my head and shoulders. I did not see my lower limbs.

' "The body leaving me was not exactly in vapour form, yet it seemed to expand very slightly once it was clear of me," says Mr. Sharpe.

' "Suddenly I am sitting on a very small object travelling at great speed, out and up into a dull, blue-grey sky at a 45-degree angle.

' "Down below me to my left I saw a pure white cloud-like substance also moving up on a line that would intersect my course.

' "It was perfectly rectangular in shape but full of holes like a sponge.

' "My next sensation was of floating in a bright pale yellow light—a very delightful feeling.

' "I continued to float, enjoying the most beautiful, tranquil sensation.

' "Then there were sledge-hammer blows to my left side. They created no actual pain, but jarred me so much that I had difficulty in retaining my balance. I began to count them and when I got to six I said aloud, 'What the ... are you doing to me?' and opened my eyes."

'He said he recognised doctors and nurses around his bed, who told him he had suffered a cardiac arrest and he had been defibrillated—shocked by electrical pulses to start his heart beating normally.

'The doctors said it was unusual for a heart-attack patient to remember events surrounding the attack and that usually there was a period of amnesia for several hours before and after an attack.'

'Well!!!' exclaimed Helen Hensbaum as she concluded her reading and sat back to gaze at the two women before her. 'How VERY interesting!' she reiterated.

Martha MacGoohoogly smirked with self-satisfied pleasure that she had shown 'the foreign woman' something she had not known before. 'Good, eh?' she smiled. 'The real Original McCoy of bunk, eh?'

Helen Hensbaum smiled in a quizzical sort of way as she asked, 'So you think this is strange, no? You think it is the—what you call it?—the bunk? No, ladies, this is ordinary. Look here, I show!' She jumped to her feet and led the way into another room. There, in a very smart bookcase reposed books. More books than Martha had ever seen in a house before.

Helen Hensbaum moved forward and picked out certain books. 'Look,' she exclaimed, riffling the pages as one handling old and beloved friends. 'Look—here is all this and more in print. The Truth. The Truth brought to us by one man who has been penalised and persecuted for telling the Truth. And now, just because some silly pressman writes an article people can believe it IS true.'

Mrs. Martha MacGoohoogly looked curiously at the titles, 'The Third Eye,' 'Doctor from Lhasa'. 'Wheressat?' she muttered before scanning the rest of the titles. Then, turning round, she exclaimed, 'You don't believe THAT stuff, do you? Cor, flip me bloomin' eyelids, that's FICTION!'

Helen Hensbaum laughed out loud. 'Fiction?' she gasped at last. 'FICTION? I have studied these books and I KNOW they are true. Since reading "You—Forever" I too can astral travel.'

Martha looked blank. 'Poor doll is mixing German with her English,' she thought. 'Astral travel? What's that? A new airline or something?' Maud just stood there with her mouth hanging open; all this was MUCH beyond her. All SHE wanted to read was the 'Sunday Supplement' with all the latest sex crimes.

'This ustral, astril travel or whatever it is, whatever is it?' asked Martha. 'Is there REALLY anything in it? Could my Old Man, who is dead and gone, God Rest His Soul, come to me and tell me where he stashed his money before he croaked?'

'Yes, I tell you. YES, it COULD be done if there was a real reason for it. If it were for the good of others—yes.'

'Heepers jeepers, cats in creepers,' ejaculated a flustered Martha. 'Now I shall be afraid to sleep tonight in case my

Old Man comes back to haunt me—and gets up to his old capers again.' She shook her head sadly as she muttered, 'He always was a great one in the bedroom!'

Helen Hensbaum poured out more tea. Martha MacGoohoogly fingered the books. 'Say, Mrs. H., would you lend me one of these?' she asked.

Mrs. Hensbaum smiled. 'No,' she replied. 'I never lend my book because an author has to live on the pitiful sum which is called a "royalty", seven per cent, it is, I believe. If I LEND books, then I am depriving an author of his living.' She lapsed into silent thought and then exclaimed, 'I'll tell you what,' she offered, 'I will BUY you a set as a gift, then you can read the Truth for yourself. Fair enough?'

Martha shook her head dubiously. 'Well, I dunno,' she said. 'I just DUNNO. I don't like the thought that when we have put away a body all tidy like, and screwed him down in his box and then shovelled him into the earth that he is going to come back all spooky like and scare the living daylights out of us.'

Maud felt rather out of things, she thought it was time for her to put in her 'two-bits worth'. 'Yes,' she said hesitantly. 'When we send him up the crematorium chimney in a cloud of greasy smoke, well, that should be the end of THAT!'

'But look,' interrupted Martha, with a cross glance at Maud. 'If, as you say, there is life after death, WHY IS THERE NO PROOF? They are gone, that is the last we hear of them. Gone—if they DID live on they would get in touch with us—God forbid!'

Mrs. Hensbaum sat silently for a moment, then rose and moved to a small writing-desk. 'Look,' she said as she returned with a photograph in her hands. 'Look at this. This is a photograph of my twin brother. He is a prisoner of the Russians, held in Siberia. We know he is alive because the Swiss Red Cross have told us so. Yet we cannot get a message from him. I am his twin and I KNOW he is alive.' Martha sat and stared at the photograph, and turned the frame over and over in her hands.

'My mother is in Germany, East Germany. She too is alive but we cannot communicate. Yet these two people are still on this Earth, still with us! And supposing you have a friend in, say, Australia whom you desire to telephone.

Even if you have his number you still have to take account of the difference in time, you have to use some mechanical and electrical contrivances. And even then you may not be able to speak to your friend. He may be at work, he may be at play. And this is just to the other side of this world. Think of the difficulties of phoning to the other side of THIS life!'

Martha started to laugh. 'Oh dear, oh dear! Mrs. Hensbaum, you are a card!' she chortled. 'A telephone, she says, to the other side of life.'

'Hey! Wait a minute, though!' suddenly exclaimed Maud in high excitement. 'Yes, sure, you have something there! My son is in electronics with the B.B.C. and he was telling us—you know how boys talk—about some old geezer who did invent such a telephone and it worked. Micro-frequencies or something it was, then it was all hushed up. The Church got in the act, I guess.'

Mrs. Hensbaum smiled her approval to Maud and added, 'Yes, it is perfectly true, this author I have been telling you about knows a lot about the matter. The device is stopped for lack of money to develop it, I believe. But anyhow, messages DO come through. There is no death.'

'Well, you prove it,' exclaimed Martha rudely.

'I can't prove it to you just like that,' mildly replied Mrs. Hensbaum, 'but look at it like this; take a block of ice and let it represent the body. The ice melts, which is the body decaying, and then we have water, which is the soul leaving.'

'Nonsense!' exclaimed Martha. 'We can see the water, but show me the soul!'

'You interrupted me, Mrs. MacGoohoogly,' responded Mrs. Hensbaum. 'The water will evaporate into invisible vapour, and THAT represents the stage of life after death.'

Maud had been fretting because the conversation was leaving her behind. After several moments of hesitation, she said, 'I suppose, Mrs. Hensbaum, if we want to get in touch with the Dear Departed we go to a seance who then put us in touch with the spirits?'

'Oh dear no!' laughed Martha, jealously guarding her position. 'If you want spirits you go to the pub and get a drop of Scotch. Old Mrs. Knickerwhacker is supposed to be a good medium, and she DOES like the other kind of spirits too. Have you ever been to a seance, Mrs. Hensbaum?'

Helen Hansbaum shook her head sadly, 'No, ladies,' she replied. 'I do not go to seances. I do not believe in them. Many of those who do go are sincere believers, but—Oh!—they are so greatly misled.' She looked at the clock and jumped to her feet in agitated alarm. '*Mein lieber Gott!*' she exclaimed. 'The lunch of my husband I should be getting already.' Recovering her composure, she continued more calmly, 'If you are interested, come along here at three this afternoon and we will talk some more, but now to my household duties I must attend.'

Martha and Maud rose to their feet and made for the door. 'Yes,' said Martha, speaking for both of them, unasked, 'we will come again at three as you suggest.'

Together they walked down the back garden, and out into the back lane. Only once did Martha speak, when they were parting. 'Well, I dunno,' she remarked. 'I really dunno. But let's meet here at ten to three. See ya!' and she turned into her door while Maud walked farther up the lane to her own abode.

In the Hensbaum house Mrs. H. swept around in a fury of controlled germanic efficiency, muttering strange words to herself, dishes and cutlery spewing from her hands to find their unerring places on the table as if she were a highly-paid juggler in a Berlin music hall. By the time the front gate clicked and the measured tread of her husband's footsteps reached the door all was ready—lunch was served.

The sun had passed its high and was angling down to the western sky when Maud emerged from her door and sauntered jauntily down towards her friend's house. A stunning apparition she was, in a flowered print dress which smacked strongly of a bargain store near Wapping Steps. 'Yoo hoo, Martha!' she called as she reached the garden door.

Martha opened the door and blinked dazedly at Maud. 'Blimey!' she said in an awed voice. 'Scrambled eggs and sunset, eh?'

Maud bristled. 'Yer skirt's too tight, Martha,' she said. 'Yer showing the lines of yer girdle and yer knickers. Who are you to talk, anyhow?'

And of a truth, Martha DID look a bit of a sight! Her two-piece pearl-grey skirt and jacket were almost indecently tight; a student of anatomy would have had no difficulty in locating the various 'landmarks' even including the *linea alba*. Her high heels were so high that she had to strut and the quite unnatural height gave her a tendency to tail-wag or behind-bounce. With her considerable endowments in the 'dairy bar' department she had to adopt a remarkable posture—like an American soldier on parade.

Together they paraded up the lane and entered the Hensbaum back garden. Mrs. Hensbaum opened the door at the first knock and ushered them in. 'My! Mrs. Hensbaum,' said Maud in some surprise as they entered the 'parlour'. 'Have you gone into the book-selling business?'

'Oh no, Mrs. O'Haggis,' smiled the German woman. 'I thought you were very interested in the psychic sciences and so I bought a set of these Rampa books for each of you as a gift from me.'

'Gee!' muttered Martha, fingering one of the books. 'Strange-looking old fellow, isn't he? Does he REALLY have a cat growing out of his head like this?'

Mrs. Hensbaum laughed outright, her face purpling in the process. '*Ach* no,' she exclaimed, 'publishers take great liberties with the covers of books; the author has no say at all in the matter. Wait—I show you——' and she dashed away up the stairs, to return somewhat breathless carrying a small photograph. 'THIS is what the author looks like. I wrote to him and he replied and sent me this, which I treasure.'

'But, Mrs. Hensbaum,' said Martha in some exasperation as they sat discussing things. 'Mrs. Hensbaum, you have no PROOF of anything. It is all FICTION.'

'Mrs. MacGoohoogly,' replied Mrs. Hensbaum, 'you are quite wrong. There IS proof, but proof which has to be experienced, to be lived. My brother is in the hands of the Russians. I told a friend of mine, Miss Rhoda Carr, that he had visited me in the astral and told me that he was at a prison named Dnepropetrovsk. He said it was a very large prison complex in Siberia. I had never heard of it. Miss Rhoda Carr said nothing then, but some weeks later she wrote to me and confirmed it. She is connected with some sort of organisation and she was in a position to make enquiries through undercover friends in Russia. But, very interestingly, she told me that many people had been able to tell her such things about their relatives in Russia and all, she said, by occult means.'

Maud was sitting with her mouth open, then she sat up straight and said, 'My mother told me that once she went to a seance and she was told some very true things. Everything she was told came true. But why do you say that these seances are no good, Mrs. Hensbaum?'

'No, I did not say that ALL of them were no good, I said I did not believe in them. On the other side of Death there are mischievous entities who can read one's thoughts and who play games with people. They read the thoughts and then give messages, pretending that it is from some Indian Guide or from some Dear Departed. Most of the messages are silly, meaningless, but sometimes, by accident, SOMETHING comes through which is fairly accurate.'

'They must blush a bit when they read MY thoughts,' sniggered Martha. 'I never was a Sunday-school girl.'

Mrs. Hensbaum smiled and continued, 'People are very misled about those who have Passed Over. There, they have work to do, they are NOT hanging round waiting—panting —to answer silly questions. THEY HAVE THEIR WORK TO DO. Would you, Mrs. O'Haggis, welcome some silly telephone call when you were extremely busy and pressed for time? Would YOU, Mrs. MacGoohoogly, welcome a nuisance at the door when you were already late for Bingo?'

'Aw, she is right, you know,' muttered Martha. 'But you said about Indian Guides. I've heard about them. WHY do they have to be Indian?'

'Mrs. MacGoohoogly, pay no attention to such tales,' answered Mrs. Hensbaum. 'People imagine Indian guides, imagine Tibetan guides, etc., etc., etc. Just think of it, here, in this life, one may regard the Indian, the Tibetan, or the Chinese as poor underprivileged coloured natives not worthy of a second thought. How, then, can we suddenly regard them as psychic geniuses as soon as they get to the Other Side? No, many most uninformed people "adopt" an Indian Guide because it is more mysterious. Actually one's ONLY guide is ... one's Overself.'

'Ah! 'Tis beyond us yer talkin', Mrs. Hensbaum. You have us lost amid the words.'

Mrs. Hensbaum laughed and replied, 'It is so, the books

you should read first maybe, starting with "The Third Eye".'

'And if I may be so bold, may we come and talk to you again?' asked Maud O'Haggis.

'Yes indeed you may, for it will be my pleasure,' replied Mrs. Hensbaum hospitably. 'Why do we not arrange to meet here at this time one week from today?'

And so a few minutes later, the two ladies were ambling along the lane again, each carrying a load of books which were the gifts of Mrs. Helen Hensbaum. 'I wish she had said a bit more about what happens when we die, though,' said Maud wistfully.

'Aw, you'll know soon enough by the look of ye,' responded Martha.

The lights burned long at the MacGoohoogly and O'Haggis residences; deep into the night a glimmer of light shone through the red blind of Martha's bedroom. At times a vagrant wind would edge aside the heavy green drapes of Maud's sitting-room to reveal her hunched up in a high chair, a book clasped tightly in her hands.

A late bus roared past, carrying night-time office cleaners back to their homes. In the distance a train clanked majestically by, the heavy load of freight cars swaying and rattling over the rails of a shunting yard. There came the wail of a syren. Police or ambulance, neither mattered to Maud deeply immersed in her book. From the Town Hall clock came the chimes and the hour-strike indicating that the morning was progressing. At last the light faded from Martha's bedroom. Soon, too, the downstairs light was extinguished from Maud's sitting-room, and for a few brief moments a glimmer of brightness appeared in her bedroom.

The clatter of the early morning milkman disturbed the peaceful scene. Soon there came the street cleaners with their trundling carts and metallic clangor. Buses swung into the street for early morning workers to board and be carried yawning to their jobs. Smoke appeared from a myriad chimneys. Doors opened briefly and slammed hurriedly as people sped forth in the daily race with time and trains.

At last the red blind of Martha's bedroom shot up with such violence that the pull-tassle was set a-dancing. The startled, sleep-bleared face of Martha stared blankly upon

18

an uncaring world. Her hair, set in tight curlers, gave her a wild, unkempt appearance, while a vast flannel nightdress accentuated her large size and more than ample endowments.

Later, at the O'Haggis house, the door slowly opened, and an arm stretched out to reach the milk bottle on the step. After a long interval, the door opened again, and Maud appeared clad in a striped housecoat. Tiredly she shook two mats, yawned violently, and withdrew again into the seclusion of her home.

A solitary cat emerged from some dark passage, peered cautiously around before venturing to walk sedately to the roadway. Right in the centre of the street he stopped, sat down and did his toilet, face, ears, paws, and tail, before ambling off into some other dark corner in search of breakfast.

CHAPTER TWO

'Timon! TIMON!' The voice was shrill, fear-laden, with that rasping intonation which jars one and sets the nerves on edge. 'Timon, WAKE UP, your father is dying.' Slowly the young boy swam back from the deeps of utter unconsciousness. Slowly he struggled through the fogs of sleep, trying to open leaden eyelids. 'Timon, you MUST wake up. YOUR FATHER IS DYING!' A hand grasped his hair and shook him violently. Timon opened his eyes. Suddenly he became aware of a strange, rasping noise, 'like a strangling yak', he thought. Curiously he sat up and swivelled his head around striving to see through the gloom of the small room.

On a small ledge stood a stone dish in which a lump of butter floated in its own turgid, melted oil. Roughly thrust into the unmelted butter a strip of coarse cloth acted as a crude wick. Now it sputtered, flared, and dimmed throwing flickering shadows on the walls behind it. A vagrant draught caused the wick to dip momentarily; it spluttered and spat, and the feeble flame became even dimmer. Then, saturated afresh by its partial immersion it flared anew, sending smoky fingers of soot across the room.

'TIMON! Your father is dying, you must hurry for the Lama!' cried his mother in desperation. Slowly, still drugged with sleep, Timon rose to his reluctant feet, and drew his solitary garment around him. The rasping noise quickened, slowed and resumed its monotonous, chilling rhythm. Timon drew near the huddled bundle at the side of which crouched his mother. Staring down with fear-filled eyes he felt numb horror at the sight of his father's face, made even more ghastly by the flickering butter lamp. Blue, he was, blue with a hard, cold look about him. Blue with the onset of cardiac failure. Tense with the signs of rigor mortis even while he yet lived.

'Timon!' said his mother. 'You must go for the Lama or your father will die with no one to guide him. Hurry, HURRY!' Whirling about, Timon dashed for the door. Outside the stars gleamed hard and cold in the darkness which comes before the dawn, the hour when Man is most prone to fail and falter. The bitter wind, chilled by the fog-banks looming over the mountain edge, swirled around, rolling small stones and whipping up clouds of fine dust.

The small boy, scarce ten years of age, stood and shivered as he strove to peer through the darkness, a darkness but poorly relieved by the faint star-glow. No moon here, this was the wrong time of the month. The mountains stood hard and black, with only the faintest of purpling to show where they ended and the sky began. From the point where a vague purple smudge swept down to the faintly glowing river, a minute speck of wavering yellow light shone the brighter because of the all-pervading darkness. Quickly the boy jumped into motion, running, jumping, hurdling fallen rocks in his overpowering anxiety to reach the sanctuary of that light.

Cruel flints slithered and stung beneath his unshod feet. Round pebbles, remnants perhaps from some ancient sea-bed, moved treacherously at his footsteps. Boulders loomed alarmingly through the blackness of the pre-dawn morning and bruised him as he grazed against them in his fear-inspired flight.

The feeble light in the distance beckoned. Behind him his father lay dying with no Lama to guide his soul's faltering steps. He sped on. Soon his breath was coming in rasping gasps in the thin mountain air. Soon his side ached with the agony of the 'stitch' which afflicts those who strive too much in running. The pain became a searing overtone to his life. Retching and sobbing as he strove to get more air, he was compelled to slow his race to a fast trot and then, for a few steps, to a limping walk.

The light beckoned, a beacon of hope in an ocean of hope-lessness. What would become of them now, he wondered. How would they live? How would they eat? Who would look after them, protect them? His heart throbbed violently until he feared that it might burst forth from his heaving chest. Perspiration poured down him, to quickly turn chill in the frigid air. His solitary garment was tattered, faded, and scant protection against the elements. They were poor, desperately poor, and likely to become even more so with the loss of the father, the wage-earner.

The light beckoned on, a refuge in an ocean of fear. Beckoned on, flickered, burned low and rose again as if to remind the lonely boy that his father's life was flickering low, but would become bright again beyond the confines of this hard world. He burst into frenzied motion again, tucking his elbows into his sides, running with his mouth wide open, exerting every muscle to save the fleeting seconds.

The light became larger, like a star welcoming him home. By his side the Happy River flowed chuckling as it made sport with the small stones it had pushed from the mountainous heights which gave it birth. The river glowed dull silver in the faint starlight. Ahead of him the boy could now faintly discern the blacker bulk of a small lamasery perched between the river and the mountainside.

Looking at the light and the river, his attention was distracted, and an ankle gave beneath him, throwing him violently to the ground, skinning hands, knees, and face. Sobbing with pain and frustration he climbed painfully to his feet and hobbled on.

Suddenly, just in front of him, a figure appeared. 'Who is abroad around our walls?' asked a deep old voice. 'Ah! And what brings you to our door at this hour of the morning?' the voice continued. Timon peering through tear-swollen eyelids saw a bent old monk before him. 'Oh! You are hurt—come inside and I will see to you,' the voice went on. Slowly the old man turned and led the way back into the small lamasery. Timon stood blinking in the sudden light of some small butter lamp—bright indeed after the darkness outside.

The air was heavy with the scent of incense. Timon stood tongue-tied for a moment and then poured out his message. 'My father, he is DYING, and my mother sent me fast to bring aid that he may be guided on his journey. He is DYING!' The poor boy sank to the floor, covering his weeping eyes with his hands. The old monk shuffled out and soon might have been heard in whispered conversation in another room. Timon sat upon the floor weeping in an ecstasy of self-pity and fright.

Soon he was roused by a fresh voice saying, 'My son! My

son! Ah, it is young Timon, yes, I know YOU, my boy.'
Timon respectfully bowed and then slowly climbed to his
feet, wiping his eyes with the corner of his robe and so
smearing moist road-side dust all over his tear-wet face.
'Tell me, my boy,' said the Lama, for that was whom
Timon recognised him to be. Once again Timon told his tale
and at its completion the Lama said, 'Come, we will go
together—I will lend you a pony. First drink this tea and
eat this tsampa, for you must be famished and the day will
be long and tiring.'

The old monk came forward with the food, and Timon
sat upon the floor to consume it while the Lama went away
to make his preparations. There came the sound of horses
and the Lama entered the room again. 'Ah, so you have
finished. Good, then let us away,' and he turned, leaving
Timon to follow him.

Now over the far edge of the mountain girding the Plain
of Lhasa the first faint golden streaks of light were
approaching, heralding the birth of a new day. Suddenly a
glint of light shone through a high mountain pass and for a
moment touched the house of Timon's parents at the far
end of the road. 'Even the day dies, my boy,' said the Lama,
'but in a few hours it is reborn as a new day. So it is with all
living things.'

Three ponies stood restlessly at the door in the very insecure care of an acolyte scarce older than Timon. 'We
have to ride these things,' the young acolyte whispered to
Timon, 'put your hands over his eyes if he won't stop. And'
—he added gloomily—'if THAT doesn't stop him, JUMP for
it.'

Quickly the Lama mounted. The young acolyte gave
Timon a hand, and then, with the leap of desperation,
jumped on his own horse and rode off after the other two
now fading into the darkness that yet covered the land.

Golden shafts of light spread across the mountain-tops as
the sun showed his topmost edge over the eastern rise.
Frozen moisture in the frigid air reflected a myriad of
colours and shades of colours from the prisms of ice. Giant
shadows raced across the land as the shades of night were
pushed aside by the relentlessly approaching day. The three
lonely travellers, mere specks of dirt in the immensity of
the barren land, rode on through the boulder-strewn

countryside, evading the rockfalls and pits the more easily for the increasing light.

Soon there could be seen a lonely figure standing at the side of the desolate house, a woman, shading her eyes, peering in anguish along the path. Hoping for the help that seemed so long in coming. The three rode on, picking a careful way amid the rock debris. 'I do not know how you managed so well, boy,' said the Lama to Timon, 'it must have been a frightening journey.' But poor Timon was too frightened and too tired to answer. Even now he swayed and drowsed on the back of the pony. The three rode on in silence.

At the door the woman stood wringing her hands and bobbing her head in a half-abashed gesture of respect. The Lama swung off his horse and went to the sorrowing woman. The young acolyte slithered off his pony and went to the aid of Timon, but too late; that young man had just toppled off as soon as the pony stopped.

'Holy Lama,' quavered the woman, 'my husband is almost gone, I have kept him conscious but I feared you would be too late. Oh! What SHALL we do?'

'Come, show me the way,' commanded the Lama, following the woman as she turned and led the way in. The house was dark. Oiled cloth covered the holes in the walls, for there was no glass here and well-oiled cloth brought from distant India served in its place, admitting a strange kind of light and a peculiar fragrance all of its own. A fragrance composed of drying-out oil well mixed with soot from the ever-smouldering butter lamp.

The floor was of well-pounded earth, and the walls were composed of heavy stones compacted together, with gaps stopped by yak dung. A small fire, the fuel of which was also yak dung, smouldered in the centre of the room and the smoke drifted up and some of it eventually escaped through a hole in the roof constructed for that purpose.

By the side of the far wall opposite the entrance there lay a bundle which at first glance might have been taken for a bundle of rags tossed aside, but the illusion was dispelled by the sounds which came from the bundle. The rasping, croaking sounds of a man struggling to keep the breath within his body, the sounds of a man in extremis. The Lama moved towards him and peered through the all-pervading

24

gloom at the one who was lying on the floor, an elderly, thin man stamped with the hardship of life, a man who had lived according to all the beliefs of his ancestors without having a thought of things for himself.

Now he lay there gasping, blue faced through lack of oxygen. He lay there sobbing out his life, striving to retain some tenuous consciousness, for his belief and traditional belief was that his journey to the other world would be the easier for the guidance of a trained Lama.

He looked up and some semblance—some fleeting look— of pleasure flitted across his ghastly features at the realisation that now the Lama was here.

The Lama sank down beside the dying man and placed his hands upon his temples, uttering soothing sounds to him. Behind him the young acolyte hurriedly set out incense burners and took some incense from a package. Then, taking from his pouch tinder, flint, and iron, he industriously set spark to tinder and blew it into flame so that the incense could be lighted when required.

Not for him the easier disrespectful system of touching the incense to the now-guttering butter lamp, that would have shown lack of thought for the incense, lack of respect for the ritual. He was going to light the incense in the traditional way, for he, that eager young man, had great ambitions of being a Lama himself.

The Lama sitting in the lotus position beside the almost moribund man on the floor, nodded to the acolyte who then lit the first stick of incense, lit it so that flame just touched the tip of the first stick and then, as it glowed red, blew it out, leaving the stick to smoulder. The Lama moved his hands slightly to a different position on the man's head and said, 'Oh Spirit about to depart from this its case of flesh, we light the first stick of incense that your attention may be attracted, that you may be guided, that you may take an easy path through the perils which your undirected imagination will place before you.'

There was a strange peace apparent on the dying man's face. Now it was bedewed with perspiration, a thin sheen of moisture, the perspiration of approaching death. The Lama gripped his head firmly and nodded slightly to the acolyte. That young man bent forward again and lit the second stick of incense, and blew out the flame, leaving the second stick of incense to smoulder.

'Oh Spirit about to depart for the Greater Reality, the True Life beyond this, your time of release has come. Be prepared to keep your consciousness fixed firmly upon me even when you leave this, your present body, for I have much to tell you. Pay attention.' The Lama moved forward again and placed his interlocked fingers on the very top of the man's head. The dying man's stertorous breathing sounded rattly, raggedy. His chest heaved and fell. Suddenly he gave a short, sharp gasp, almost a cough, and his body arched upwards until it was supported by the back of his head and his heels. For what seemed to be an interminable time he stayed thus, a rigid bow of flesh and bone. Then all of a sudden the body jerked, jerked upwards so that it was perhaps an inch, perhaps two inches, from the ground. Then it collapsed, sagged like a half-empty sack of wheat thrown carelessly aside. A last despairing wheeze of air escaped from the lungs, the body twitched and was still, but from within there came the gurgle of fluids, the rumbling of organs, and the settling of joints.

The Lama nodded again to the acolyte, who, waiting, immediately touched flame to the third stick of incense and set it to smoulder with flame extinguished in the third incense holder. 'Spirit now released from the suffering body, pay attention before setting out on your journey, pay attention for by your faulty knowledge, your faulty imaginings, you have set snares which can impede the comfort of this, your journey. Pay attention, for I shall detail to you the steps you must take and the Path you must follow. Pay attention.'

Outside the small room the morning wind was rising as the poor heat of the sun's rays, tipping over the mountain edge, started to disturb the cold of the long night, and with the first rays of even that faint warmth air currents rose up from the cold ground and disturbed little eddies of dust which now swirled and rattled against the oiled cloth openings of the room until it sounded to the frightened woman watching from the doorway almost as if Devils were rattling and trying to get at her husband, now lying dead before her.

She thought of the enormity of it. One moment she was married to a living man, a man who for years had provided

26

for her, a man who had assured such security as there ever could be in her life, but at the next moment he was dead, dead, lying dead before her on the earth floor of their room. She wondered what would become of her now. Now she had nothing but a son who was too young to work, too young to earn, and she suffering from a sickness which sometimes came upon women who were denied assistance at the time of their child's birth. She had dragged herself around for the whole number of years of her son's age.

The Lama kneeling beside the body on the floor, closed the eyes of the corpse and placed little pebbles on the shut lids to keep them closed. He put a band under the chin and tied it at the top of the head to keep the sagging jaw tight so that the mouth should be shut. Then, at a signal from him, the fourth stick of incense was lit and placed carefully in its holder. Now there were four sticks of incense and the smoke from them trailed upwards almost as if they had been drawn in blue-grey chalk, so straight were the pillars of smoke in the almost airless room without draught.

The Lama spoke again, 'Oh departed Spirit of the body before us, the fourth stick of incense has been lit to draw your attention and to hold you here while I talk, while I tell you of that which you will find. Oh Spirit about to wander, heed my words that your wanderings may be directed.'

The Lama looked sadly at the corpse, thinking of the training that he had had. He was telepathic, clairaudient, he could see the aura of the human body, that strange, coloured —multi-coloured—flame which swirled and wove about a living body. Now, as he looked at the dead body, he could see that the flame was almost extinguished. There was, instead of the colours of the rainbow and many more besides, just an eddying grey-blue turning darker. But streaming from the body, the grey-blue moved upwards to about two feet above the corpse. There, there was active motion, violent motion, it looked like many fire-flies darting about, fire-flies who had been trained as soldiers and who were endeavouring to find their preordained places. The little particles of light moved, swirled, and interwove, and before the Lama's eyes, before his third eye, there appeared soon a replica of the corpse, but as a living man, a young man. It was tenuous as yet, floating naked about two feet above the body. It rose and fell slightly, perhaps two or three inches

27

at a time. It rose and fell, regained its position, fell and rose, and all the time the details were becoming more clear, the filmy body was filling out and becoming more substantial.

The Lama sat and waited while the greyish-blue light of the dead body became dimmer, but while the multi-coloured light composing the body above became stronger, more substantial, more vivid. At last there was a sudden swelling and a jerk and the 'ghost' body tipped with its head up and its feet down. The very slight joining between the dead flesh and the living spirit parted and the spirit was now complete and living independent of its former host-body. Immediately there came into that little room the odour of death, the strange, spicy odour of a body starting to decay, an unpleasant odour which rather stung the nostrils high up between the eyes.

The young acolyte, sitting behind the smouldering sticks of incense, carefully rose to his feet and went to the open door. Bowing ceremoniously to the new widow and her son, Timon, he gently ushered them out of the room and shut the door firmly. Standing with his back to the door, he paused a moment to utter, whispering to himself, 'Phew! What a fug!!' Softly he moved to the oil-cloth covering the window opening and eased away one corner to let in fresh air. A whole torrent of wind-blown sand poured in and left him sputtering and coughing.

'SHUT THAT WINDOW!' said the Lama in subdued but still ferocious tones. Peering through almost closed eyes the acolyte fumbled blindly at the now-flapping cloth and managed to wedge it over the frame again. 'Well, at least I got a breath of fresh air, better than THIS stink!' he thought to himself before returning to his place and resuming his seat again behind the four sticks of smoking incense.

The body lay inert upon the floor. From it there came the gurgling of fluids ceasing their flow and finding their own levels. There came too the rumbling and groaning of organs giving up life, for a body does not die on the instant, but in stages, organ by organ. First is the death of the higher centres of the brain and then, in orderly procession, other organs, finally deprived of the direction of the brain, cease to function, cease to produce those secretions or pass on the substance which is necessary for the continuation of that complex mechanism referred to as a body.

As the life force withdraws it leaves the confines of the body and assembles outside, congregating in an amorphous mass just above the body. It hovers by magnetic attraction while there is yet some life, while there is yet some flow of life particles departing their former host. In time, as more and more organs give up their life force, the tenuous form floating above the flesh-body comes more and more to resemble it. At last, when the resemblance was complete, the magnetic attraction would have ceased and the 'spirit body' would float off on its next journey.

Now the spirit was complete and held to the dead body by only the most fragile of threads. It floated, and the spirit itself was confused and terrified. Being born to life on the Earth was a traumatic experience. That meant dying to another form of existence. Dying on Earth meant that the spirit body was being born again on another world, on the spirit world, or one of them. Now the form hovered, floated higher and sank lower, floated, and awaited the instruction of the telepathic Lama, one whose whole life was devoted to helping those who were leaving Earth.

The Lama watched carefully, using his telepathic senses to assess the capacity of the newly released spirit and his third eye to actually view its form. At least he broke the silence with telepathic instruction. 'Oh newly released spirit,' said the Lama, 'pay attention to my thoughts that your passage may be eased thereby. Heed the instructions which I shall give that your path may be smoothed, for millions have trod this path before you and millions more will follow.'

The floating entity, so recently a fairly alert man of the Earth, stirred slightly. A dim greenish hue suffused its being. A faint ripple ran its whole length and then it subsided again into inertia. But there was an awareness, although ill-defined, that this entity was now on the brink of awakening from the coma of translation from death on Earth to birth in the spirit plane.

The Lama watched, studying, assessing, estimating. At last he spoke, telepathically, again, saying, 'Oh Spirit newly liberated from the bonds of the flesh, hear me. A fifth stick of incense is lit to attract your wandering attention that you may be guided.' The young acolyte had been brooding on the problem of how to get out and play. THIS was ideal kite-flying weather. Others were out—why not he? Why had he to ... but now he jumped to attention and hastily lit the fifth stick of incense, blowing out the flame with such energy that the red-glowing stick promptly burst into flame again.

The smoke wafted upwards and wove tenuous fingers around the gently undulating spirit figure floating above the dead body. The young acolyte resumed his consideration on the problems of kite-flying. A cord attached a little further back, he pondered, would give a greater angle of attack to the air and would give a faster climb. But if he did that ... his deliberations were again interrupted by the words of the Lama.

'Oh liberated Spirit,' intoned the Lama, 'your soul must become alert. Too long have you wilted under the superstitions of the ignorant. I bring you knowledge. The sixth stick of incense is lit to bring you knowledge for you must know yourself ere starting on your journey.' The acolyte scrabbled frantically on the dim, earth floor for the stick which he had just dropped, and muttered an exclamation NOT taught in the lamasery as his probing fingers encountered the smouldering tinder, and just beyond it, the unlit stick. Hastily he ignited it and thrust it in the incense holder.

The Lama glanced disapprovingly at him and continued his instruction to the Departing Spirit. 'Your life from the cradle to the grave has been enmeshed in superstition and false fears. Know that many of your beliefs are without foundation. Know that many of the devils you fear will haunt you are of your own making. The seventh stick of incense is lit to bind you here that you may be adequately instructed and prepared for the journey ahead.' The acolyte was ready, the incense was lit and left a-smoulder, and the Lama continued his exhortation and instruction.

'We are but puppets of the One who is Higher, put down on Earth that He may experience the things of Earth. We sense but dimly our immortal birthright, our eternal associations, and sensing so dimly we imagine, we fear, and we rationalise.' He ceased and watched the silent cloud-figure before him. Watched, and saw the gradual awakening, the quickening into awareness. Sensed the panic, the uncertainty, felt a measure of the dreadful shock from one torn from his familiar places and things. Sensed, and understood.

The spirit-form dipped and swayed. The Lama spoke to it, 'Speak with your thoughts. I shall receive those thoughts if you emerge from the stupor of shock. THINK that you are able to talk to me.' The spirit-form pulsed and wavered; ripples undulated throughout its length, then, like the first faint cheep of a bird newly hatched from the egg, came the wail of a frightened soul.

'I am lost in the wilderness,' it said, 'I am afraid of all the devils who beset me. I fear those who would hale me to the nether regions and burn me or freeze me throughout eternity.' The Lama clucked in sympathy, and then said, 'Spirit affrighted for naught. Listen to me. Put aside your needless fears and listen to me. Give me your attention that I may guide you and bring you solace.'

'I hear you, Holy Lama,' the spirit-form made rejoinder, 'and I will attend upon your words.'

The Lama nodded to the young acolyte who thereupon seized a stick of incense. 'Oh affrighted Spirit,' intoned the Lama, 'the eighth stick of incense is lit that you may be guided.' The acolyte hastily thrust the smouldering tinder at the incense, and satisfied with the result, placed it firmly in the holder, leaving one vacancy yet to fill.

'Man upon the Earth,' said the Lama, 'is an irrational figure given to believing that which is not so in preference to that which is. Man is greatly given to superstition and to false beliefs. You, Spirit, fear that devils surround you. Yet there are no devils save those which your thoughts have constructed and which will vanish as a puff of smoke in a high wind if you recognise the truth. About you there are elementals, mindless forms which but reflect your thoughts of terror as a still pool will reflect your features as you bend over it. These elementals are mindless, they are but creatures of the moment like the thoughts of a drunken man. Have no fear, there is naught to harm you.'

The spirit-form whimpered with terror and said, telepathically, 'But I SEE devils, I SEE gibbering monsters who poke their taloned hands in my direction. They will devour me. I see the features of those whom I wronged in life and who now come to exact retribution.'

But the Lama raised his hands in benediction and said,

'Spirit, pay attention to me. Gaze firmly at the worst of your imagined tormentors. Gaze at him sternly, and make the strong thought that he be gone. Visualise him vanishing in a puff of smoke and he will so vanish, for he exists only in your fevered imagination. Think, NOW, I command you!'

The spirit-form heaved and wavered. Its colours flared through the whole gamut of the spectrum and then there came the triumphant telepathic shout, 'IT WENT—THEY HAVE GONE!' The spirit-form wavered, expanded and contracted, expanded and contracted, just like a man of the Earth panting after great exertion.

'There is naught to fear save fear,' said the Lama. 'If you fear not, then NOTHING can harm you. Now I will tell you what comes next and then you must go on the continuing stage of your journey towards the Light.' The spirit-form was now glowing with new colours, now it was showing confidence and the cessation of fear. Now it waited to know what lay before it.

'Now is the time,' the Lama said, 'for you to continue with your journey. When I release you you will feel a strong urge to drift. Resist it not. The currents of Life will carry you along through swirling clouds of fog. Horrid faces will peer at you through the murk, but fear them not—at your bidding they will go away. Keep your thoughts pure, your mien calm. Soon you will come to a pleasant green sward where you will feel the joy of living. Friendly helpers will come to you and make you welcome. Fear not. Respond to them, for here you CANNOT meet those who would harm you.'

The spirit-form swayed gently as it considered all these remarks. The Lama continued, 'Soon they will escort you as friends to the Hall of Memories, that place which is the repository of all knowledge, where every act, either good or bad, ever done by any person, is recorded. At the Hall of Memories you will enter and you alone will see your life as it was and as it should have been. You and you alone will judge of the success or otherwise of your endeavours. There is no other judgement, there is no hell save that which your guilty conscience will impose upon you. There is no eternal damnation, nor torments. If you have failed in your life, then you and you alone may decide to return later to the Earth life and make another attempt.'

The Lama stopped and motioned to the acolyte who thereupon took up the last stick of incense. 'Oh Spirit now instructed,' said the Lama, 'go forth upon your journey. Travel in peace. Travel knowing that you have naught to fear but fear itself. Go FORTH!' Slowly the spirit-form rose, paused a moment while the figure took a last look around the room, then it penetrated the ceiling of the room and vanished from human sight. The Lama and the acolyte rose to their feet, picked up their equipment, and left the room.

Later, as the sun was reaching its zenith, a ragged figure approached the little house and entered. Soon he emerged again carrying upon his back the swathed figure which was the mortal remains of the father of Timon. Along the stony path he trudged, bearing the body to the place whence it would be dismembered and broken so that the birds of the air, the vultures, could feed upon the remains, and in the fullness of time return the changed remnants of the body to Mother Earth.

CHAPTER THREE

'Haw! Haw! HAW!' The room rattled to the gusty guffaw. The thin young man sitting hunched up, with his back to the laughter, jerked as though he had been shot. 'Hey, Juss!' snorted the voice. 'Have you read THIS?' Mr. Justin Towne carefully covered the portable organ which he had been so lovingly fondling, and stood up.

'Read what?' he enquired crossly.

Mr. Dennis Dollywogga smiled broadly as he waved a book above his head. 'Oh boy!' he exclaimed. 'This guy thinks that all us homos are sick! He thinks we have glandular troubles, he thinks we are all mixed up between men and women. Haw! Haw! HAW!'

Justin strolled across the room and took the book from his friend. It came open at page 99, where overfolding in an ecstasy of hilarity had cracked the spine binding. Dennis peered over his friend's shoulder and extended a long pointed finger to indicate a certain passage. 'There!' he said. 'It starts THERE. Read it out, Juss, the guy must be a real square john.' He moved to a low settee and reclined limply upon it, with one arm thrown carelessly across the back. Justin polished the lens of his spectacles, replaced them upon his nose, and tucking his handkerchief back in his sleeve, picked up the book and read:

'In the hurly-burly of getting from the astral world to that world we call Earth, mix-ups occur. Being born is a traumatic experience, it's a most violent affair, and a very delicate mechanism can easily become deranged. For example, a baby is about to be born and throughout the pregnancy the mother has been rather careless about what she was eating and what she was doing, so the baby has not received what one might term a balanced chemical input.

34

The baby may be short of a chemical and so development of certain glands may have been halted. Let us say the baby was going to come as a girl, but through lack of certain chemicals the baby is actually born a boy, a boy with the inclinations of a girl.

'The parents might realise that they've got a sissyfied little wretch and put it down to over-indulgence or something, they may try to beat some sense into him one end or the other to make him more manly, but it doesn't work; if the glands are wrong, never mind what sort of attachments are stuck on in front, the boy is still a girl in a boy's body.

'At puberty the boy may not develop satisfactorily, or again, he may to all outward appearances. At school he may well appear to be one of the limp-wristed fraternity, but the poor fellow can't help that.

'When he reaches man's estate he finds he cannot "do the things that come naturally", instead he runs after boys—men. Of course he does because all his desires are the desires of a woman. The psyche itself is female, but through an unfortunate set of circumstances the female has been supplied with male equipment, it might not be much use but it is still there!

'The male then becomes what used to be called a "pansy" and has homosexual tendencies. The more the psyche is female, the stronger will be the homosexual tendencies.

'If a woman has a male psyche, then she will not be interested in men but will be interested in women, because her psyche, which is closer to the Overself than is the physical body, is relaying confusing messages to the Overself and the Overself sends back a sort of command, "Get busy, do your stuff." The poor wretched male psyche is obviously repelled by the thought of "doing his stuff" with a man, and so all the interest is centred on a female, so you get the spectacle of a female making love to a female, and that is what we call a lesbian because of a certain island off Greece where that used to be "The done thing".

'It is quite useless to condemn homosexuals, they are not villains, instead they should be classed as sick people, people who have glandular troubles, and if medicine and doctors had the brains they were born with then they would do something about that glandular defect.

'After my own experiences of late I am even more convinced that Western doctors are a crummy lot of kooks just out to make a fast buck. My own experiences have been unmentionably and adjectivally deplorable, however we are not discussing me now, we are discussing homosexuals.

'If a lesbian (woman) or a homosexual (male) can find a sympathetic doctor, then glandular extracts can be given which certainly improve the condition a lot and make life bearable, but unfortunately nowadays with the present breed of doctors who seem to be out to make money only, well, you have to search a long way to get a good doctor. But it is useless to condemn a homosexual, it is not his fault or her fault. They are very very unhappy people because they are confused, they don't know what has happened to them, and they can't help what is, after all, the strongest impulse known to man or woman—the reproduction impulse.

'Head shrinkers, alias psychologists, are not much help really because they take years to do what the average person would do in a few days. If it is clearly explained to the homosexuals that they have a glandular imbalance, then they can usually adjust. Anyhow, the laws are being amended to cater for such cases instead of subjecting them to such fierce persecution and imprisonment for what is truly an illness.

'There are various ways of helping such people. The first is that a very understanding and much older person who has deep sympathy with the sufferer should explain precisely what has happened. The second is the same as the first but with the addition that the victim should be given some medicament which suppresses the sexual urge, the sexual drive. The third—well, again, matters should be explained, and a qualified doctor can give hormone or testrone injections which can definitely help the body in the matter of sexual adjustment.

'The vital thing is that one should never, never condemn a homosexual, it's not his fault, he is being penalised for something he hasn't done, he is being penalised for some fault of Nature; perhaps his mother had the wrong sort of food, perhaps the mother and the child were chemically imcompatible. However, whichever way you look at it, homosexuals can only be helped by true understanding and sympathy, and possibly with the judicious administration of drugs.'

'What is the book?' asked Justin as he finished reading, flipping shut the cover he read out, 'Lobsang Rampa, "Feeding the Flame". He SHOULD feed the flame if he attacks us,' he commented sourly.

'What do you think of it, eh, Juss?' asked Dennis hesitantly. 'Do you think there is anything in it or is he just a guy drumming up hatred against us? What do you think, eh, Juss?'

Justin carefully smoothed his top lip where the moustache would not grow, and replied in a somewhat high voice, 'Well, isn't this fellow an ex-monk or something? He probably does not know the difference between a man and a woman, anyhow.'

They sat together upon the settee flicking through the pages of the book. 'Lot of other things he writes here make good sense, though,' mused Justin Towne. 'How come then that he is so wrong about us?' interposed Dennis Dollywogga. Then a positively brilliant thought struck him; he beamed like the newly risen sun and smiled, 'Why don't YOU write to him, Juss, and tell him he's all wet? Wait a minute, does he give an address in this book? No? Then I guess he will get it care of the publisher. Let's do it, Juss, eh?'

So it came to pass that in the fullness of time, as they say in the best circles, Author Rampa received a letter from a gentleman who insisted that Author Rampa did not know the first thing about homosexuals. Author Rampa duly considered the dire warnings about his sanity, perceptions, etc., and wrote an invitation to his correspondent. 'Admittedly I know little of ANY sexual activities,' indited the Author, 'but I still maintain the accuracy of my remarks. However,' the letter continued, 'you write me YOUR opinion of homosexuality and if my publisher has strong nerves and a good heart he will permit me to print your letter or article in my thirteenth book.'

Two heads came together. Four eyes scanned the letter which had just been delivered. 'GEE!' breathed Dennis Dollywogga in astonishment. 'The old guy has passed the ball back to us. Now what'll we do?'

Justin Towne sucked in his breath and his stomach. 'Do?' he queried in a quavery voice. 'Why, YOU will write a reply, that's what YOU'LL do. You started this.' For some time there was silence between them. Then both went off to what should have been their work but really was a session of cerebration on the boss's time.

The hands of the clock crawled slowly around the dial. At last it was time to leave work and return to 'the pad'. Dennis was first home, soon followed by Justin. 'Juss,' muttered Dennis as he chewed the last of the hamburger. 'Juss, YOU are the brains of this outfit, I am the brawn. Howsabout YOU writing some stuff. Gee, I've been thinking about it all day and I haven't scratched out a thing.'

So Justin sat down with a typewriter and knocked out a reply. Dennis read it through carefully. 'WOND-er-ful!' he gusted. 'Howsabout that!' Carefully they folded the several pages and Dennis strolled out to the mail-box.

Canada's postal services would never set a record for speed, what with strikes, sit-ins, slow-downs, and work-to-rules, but before mildew actually formed on the paper Author Rampa had the package dropped through his letter-box along with sixty-nine other letters that day. At last he came to that particular package. Slitting open the envelope he drew out the pages and read. 'Hmmm,' he said at last (if 'Hmmm' can be construed as saying). 'Well, I'll print the whole lot, letter and article because then people will have the whole thing straight from the horse's mouth.'

Later, Author Rampa returned to a re-reading of the letter and article. Turning to Miss Cleopatra the Siamese, he remarked, 'Well, Clee, in my opinion this ABSOLUTELY justifies what I wrote before. What do YOU think?' But Miss Cleopatra had other things, such as food, on her mind, so the Author just put the letter and article ready for the Publisher and here it is for you to read:

'Dear Dr. Rampa,

'I have broken a rule of mine, so to speak, by enclosing an unfinished piece of work. By that I mean that it is the First writing, off the top of my head. It is not what I wanted to say exactly, but for some reason it seems important that I get it off to you. When you see that I cannot spell and know little of English grammer you may just throw it away in disgust (I wouldn't blame you and I would not be angry).

'It does not always say well what I was trying to get across, and if I thought I would have time I would edit and rewrite it over and over until it was as good as I could make it, but perhaps it will be of some use even the way it is.

'Some of the things I wanted very much to say were: Most homos are not the little pansies you see on the street, they are not the ones the psychiatrists and doctors write about because those are the emotionally disturbed ones.

'Being an adventurer I have worked in cities, farms, some rodio work, etc., etc., and I know homos in all fields who are as normal as "blue-berry pie" so to speak. So, they can be very masculine, they can think and act like men and do NOT think and act like women or have any of the feminine characteristics which so many heterosexuals seem to think they do.

'I wanted to stress TO the homo, what an important part he could play in this world, if he'd get off his behind and quit feeling sorry for himself. I don't believe in things like this "Gay Liberation" thing where like all youngsters today they think they have to make a big issue of it, but merely go along and do one's own job well, with the tools they have (Being their own talents etc.).

'I tried to point out too that in my own case I came from a very good normal home, no hang-ups to make me emotionally disturbed, and that really no one knows or suspects me of being "Gay" unless I want to tell them ... I am NOT ashamed of it in the least, I just don't feel that it's their business any more than if I'm a Democrat or a Republican, a Christian or a hot-in-tot ... I know too that I'm luckier than many because all people immediately want to pour out their hearts to me and I have thus learned so much, so very much about peoples feelings.

'But anyway, just for the record ... You may use any or all of this article that you might want to, you may edit or change or correct or deleet it to your hearts content, or you can junk it if its not worth using and I will not be hurt. If you want a name, you can use "Justin" and if by some SLIM chance (Because I'm disappointed in it) you should want to use ANY OR PART OF IT, AND IF YOU SHOULD (sorry about the caps) need to refer me to anyone with an honest enquiry either for or opposed, I wouldn't mind writing them, but I do not have a private box number so I'd rather have an opportunity to write them first. It always seems that through no fault of my own, that through pre-destination people would suddenly meet me and it was like I was meant to be there to help ... But now, I am helping a lot of people, but not my own kind so to speak.

'Well, I guess that's about it ... I would like some day to write a book of my life (as would thousands of others) because it seems to stimulate many people to try harder, but perhaps when I'm older. Right now I'm very busy building a business, a home, and doing lots of fun things (Gardening, for example, is fun for me) we have a little place in the country with lots of wildlife and much work, I wish you were able to visit, you'd like it I think.

'I hope all is going better for you and your projects.

Sincerely, JUSTIN.

'Everyone will agree that the characteristics of each individual from every other individual are as varied as the stars in the sky or the pebbles on a beach. It is agreed, I think, that this is what makes the world what it is, what makes great men and small men, causes nations to rise and fall, and what attracts or repels one person to another. For the sake of clarity, let us agree that the word "Characteristics" implies all individual traits, moods, strengths and weaknesses, faults, gifts, and generally the sum total of what makes each individual different from all other individuals. Some of these characteristics come with us at birth either because we have developed them in previous lives or because we have chosen them as needs to help us in this life to become a more complete person. So also some of these characteristics have been developed during this lifetime.

'Societies at various times and in various places consider different characteristics to be good or bad, an asset or a detriment or just too common to be considered depending upon the particular views and needs of that particular society. But let us not deal with particular societies, but work on the teachings of all great religions, that being, that each man comes to earth expressly to learn and experience specific things, that he comes to earth deliberately choosing those characteristics which he alone needs to develop himself. This then causes us to look at all men with greater understanding, more tolerance and makes the statement "Judge not, lest ye be judged" far more significant. This is not to say that man's life is entirely pre-destined, for his free will exceeds the power of his birthright "Individual-Characteristics", and thus he may choose to use or misuse this Birthright at will.

'Of the many Characteristics possessed by man, those of an emotional nature usually seem to be the strongest. They include in part his likes and dislikes, his wants, and his loves, etc. Of these his loves or that emotional involvement which is brought on by his loves or hates and those around him play an extremely important part in his development in all other phases of his growth. For example, a man may love his chosen work to such an extent that all other experiences in life are put aside. He may love his family to such an extent that he will sacrifice his own development to assure them of their wants and needs. By the same token a man might hate to such an extent as to expend all his energies to eliminating that which he hates, forgetting entirely all that he was meant to do. Now this is particularly true in his loves and hates of another individual and when these emotional characteristics are joined by the most damaging of all, that of fear, all havoc can take place, reasoning can be lost and a complete breakdown can occur. For example, a suitor suddenly discovers his lady fair has another suitor who seems to be winning the battle, his love for her suddenly becomes even more intense, his fear of losing her magnifies his dislike for his competitor and if he allows himself, he might even forget his battle to win his love and concentrate solely on eliminating his foe by slander, trickery, and many other more drastic methods. Or he may brood and expend all his energies in feeling sorry for himself but not without turning his fears and hates secretly against his foe, but this again takes all his energies so that quite often his work will suffer, his health, his happiness, and generally all his growth will suffer.

'These then, Love and Fear and their counterparts hate and understanding (For no man can fear that which he entirely understands) are the strongest of all characteristics in man. Never are these stronger than in religious beliefs, political beliefs, and in one's personal loves. Cultures, governments, cities, towns, and small groups are all swayed and governed by their attitudes towards these predominant characteristics.

'Let us consider that which is very close and important to almost every human being. His individual love for another individual and its effect on others. "Love is blind" : "There's no accounting for taste in love" and "Love conquers all" : are all very valid statements ... John and Mary fall in love and marry against their families' wishes and a life time of misery and antagonism can be created for every member of both families. But let us not be concerned with individuals but with a universal and more dramatic difference. Let us take the difference between the Heterosexual and the Homosexual. The Heterosexual (male or female) is born into a world which seems to operate out of sheer need in a Heterosexual manner ... It's quite obvious that this is the normal pattern for procreation, etc. Thus the Heterosexual cannot fathom the reasoning of a Homosexual. Some feel the Homosexual is a degenerate, a lustful person who cannot control his or her desires; others think they are sick, etc. ... There have been hundreds of books written on the subject and most by Psychiatrists who think they (the homosexual) should have their heads shrunk, or by medical doctors who feel their plumbing should be changed or medical aids should be applied to CHANGE THEM and a few books have been written by Homosexuals who are trying desperately to defend themselves and make something out of their sometimes unhappy lives. Unfortunately, because feelings run high among the majority of uninformed Heterosexuals, there can be no list of who's who in the Homosexual world ... But for anyone informed, it's a very long list. Like all groups of people we can subdivide them and categorise the homosexuals into three main groups, one group are those as described in "Feeding the Flame" that being those who by accident in birth became as they are. The second are those who because after birth have strong emotional problems and turn to homosexuality to solve or ease those problems. It is these groups that the doctors and psychiatrists write about. Those two groups are very small in proportion to the Third and most important group. This group are those individuals who could not possibly learn all

42

that they must learn without being Homosexuals. In other words, they chose to come to this earth in this life as Homosexual.

'Before we go into that, let us first be aware of the fact that there are millions of Homosexuals in the world ... Men and Women ... Some of the world's finest have been homosexuals ... But the average person has no idea that so many of their friends and heroes and leaders are not of the same thinking that they are. In certain cities in the West the percentage is as high as ten per cent. Some surveys report even higher. In rural areas the percentage seems smaller, usually because the young homosexual girl or boy must find their own kind and since everyone knows all about everyone in a small community, it takes a lot for a person to remain in hostile country. The average person feels they can spot a homosexual any time or any place, but this is not true, even among homosexuals this is not true. There are thousands of happily married men and women with very fine children who are homosexuals and who may or may not actively "act out" as the psychiatrists like to say. It is also false that a homosexual cannot make love to the opposite sex. (There are always a few exceptions to every rule.) But the homosexual does not have sex with the opposite sex usually because there is no attraction, no interest, they feel more like brothers and sisters towards the opposite sex ... or just as friends. You will find few homosexuals who have not had sex with the opposite sex because in growing up they go through great hell, accepting the fact that they chose to be what they are ... so they feel it necessary to at least prove to themselves that they could if they wanted to ... and also to prove that they are right ... in that, physically it might be fun, but without that emotional "Rightness" it is a wrong and a waste of time, just as it's a waste of time to play football if you don't like football. Many homosexuals are very sensitive people, they USUALLY HAVE A STRONG SENSE of morality and will not hop from bed to bed (except when young—and that applies to the heterosexual world also) ... They have an eternal search for a permanent lover ... once found, their lives are no different from the heterosexual.

'Why would anyone choose to be born a homosexual? Because unlike any other group, certain things can be learned. If one chose to be born black in an all-white country, or white in an all-black community, one could learn how it feels to be in a minority group and learn things and feel things etc. that he could not as one of the masses in that group. So also the Homosexuals, except that the homosexual has a whole different set of problems to solve ... For example, he can be put in jail just for being himself (in some places) he can lose his job, he can be run out of town and can be subjected to a whole lot of very uncomfortable scenes by a very unenlightened heterosexual world. The unenlightened heterosexual world feels they are just, because to them this person is going against the laws of man and God ... But let me state here very definitely that (1) if it were God's will that he be such how can it be against His will? (2) Contrary to the belief of most NO man can be *made* a homosexual if he isn't one, any more than any man can be made a heterosexual if he isn't one. True, any man or woman can try anything ... they might even participate for a short period of time, witness the hustler and the prostitutes who will do anything for money, but these are not what we are talking about ... No mother or father need ever fear that their son or daughter is suddenly going to be Made into something else ... I have lived a long time and my life is that of a homosexual and I have spent a large part of that life working with the young on this very problem. But more of that later ... But never have I seen a happy conversion or a permanent one from one to the other. If the "Magic" which attracts one human being to another isn't there no one can make it appear. If you could, there would be almost no homosexuals in this world, because the hell they go through in growing up is so intense that they would offer anything to make that magic appear. But there is a much happier side to all this. For the homosexual can learn and develop and accomplish things he could not possibly learn otherwise.

'For the average homosexual, who once accepts himself in the right light, the greatest gift he receives is Understanding ... He has developed through his own life-experiences a strong sensitivity to the feelings of others, he or she usually has a very strong moral sense because of the monumental soul searching needed to accept oneself under these conditions. He is able to do a great deal of good in this world because he has learned the need for discretion, the need for truth, the need for an alert mind, the ability to "phsyc" out people quickly and accurately and to be able to assess a situation immediately. After all, his whole life has depended on this ability. Thus great leaders, warriors, businessmen, doctors, and every field on this earth has been aided by gifts of the homosexual. The Homosexual is usually given a great artistic and aesthetic gift or ability in which case they become writers, musicians, artists, they usually are sympathetic people, with a strong love of people as a whole thus they are great comforters.

'Consequently with all these assets plus the fact that they are (if they wish to be) undetectable, they can travel through this world as can everyone else, doing much, much good, unimpeded as would perhaps a man born with a physical defect or a mental defect be, which might cause people to shun him. Thus if the homosexual will, he can make many many points for himself in his development.

'For the record also, the crime rate among homosexuals is very very low. They are tolerant and not prone to physical violence, it is extremely rare to hear of rapes in the homosexual world ... seduction perhaps, but even then it is rare in relation to the heterosexual world, primarily because the homosexual has a great need to love and be loved and this cannot be found in rape or unwilling seduction. All in all the homosexual is not that villainous letcher that so many uninformed heterosexuals believe him to be. So often it's just that they cannot fathom why anyone could love someone of their own sex. But look at it this way; in some incarnations it is necessary to be born a woman to learn certain things, the next time one might be born a male. Thus it is the person that counts, not the physical body that they occupy. Granted all the physical senses may ordinarily attract opposite sexes in this world so that the population doesn't come to a screeching halt, but by the same token we are usually attracted to people who are a compliment to our personality and whom we feel are going to help us along the path of life and someone whom we can help along that path ... So does the homosexual.

'Perhaps if I briefly tell you a little about myself you can more readily appreciate this view.

'Born in a small California town of ideal parents. We

were quite poor, it is true, but an amazing mother and staunch Christian never allowed us to think or feel "Poor". We were rich and very lucky, after all who else when it rained could sail sailboats down their living-room floor while their mother read them exciting sea stories? Who else had parents who could go out of an evening with their rifles and in the matter of an hour bring home fresh rabbit instead of having to eat ordinary store-bought meat? We were lucky children, the three of us, and happy. Raised in a mission school (co-educational) my mother's fondest wish was for one of us to join a religious Order. By the time I was five I knew that my brother and I had different ideas on the value of girls. Within the next couple of years I knew that nothing was more attractive and pleasurable than being in the company of boys or men, I would marvel at the physical beauty of the male and I made it a point even at that age to boy-watch, and that meant being one of them (I mean to participate in their activities and join them), but always I knew that my reason for liking them was different than their reason for liking me, to them I was just one of the guys, to me they were something very special, but I wasn't quite sure why ... I could understand the girls drooling over them, but I felt sorry for the girls because they could never be a boy like me and be one of them at the same time. I never ever wanted to be a girl. Naturally as youngsters we experimented with our toys, once we learned there was more to them than originally met the eye. Again I knew I was different because of how I "felt" about it. And even then I was always shocked to learn that to the other boy the experiment meant nothing ... because to me it was as spiritual as church. This bothered me because the dear holy Nuns and the church taught that all this was very bad indeed and I offered up Masses, Prayers, Candy, Work, and all sorts of things begging to make me like everyone else. Not because I wanted to, but so many people told me I was wrong ... Not in so many words, mind you, because I KNEW I couldn't dare tell them really how I felt. I had always been a listener so I could understand them better, and I knew ...

'At thirteen I was accepted into a monastery where I hoped to please my mother by being a monk, however I knew it wasn't right and left after a year and a half. I was then on my own, because my family let me know they could not support me. This was the Depression. This meant I did not have to go to school unless I wanted to because I had to work, and of course being a normal healthy boy I didn't want to go to school (I'd never been too good at it anyway). Off to the big city to make my fortune, for a while I was going to be a sailor and sail the seven seas, I even stowed away on a tanker, but common sense (or fear) made me get off before the ship sailed, then for a while I was going to Arizona to fight Indians and bad men, I loved horses and had a way with them so I'd be good in a passe, but the thought of chasing men whom I might like put me off that venture. Being venturesome I was constantly on the move, looking for a special friend and new discoveries. By the time I was sixteen I had learned three very important things. First, everyone, men, women, and children were attracted to me in every way. In addition, everyone trusted me and confided in me, and I was a listening post and a comforter for almost everyone I met. This led me into almost every walk of life, my friends (some of them still), were wealthy, poor, crooks, and priests.

'Secondly, I learned I was Homosexual, I tried to force myself into a heterosexual life (sexually) but it always seemed unclean, whereas with my own kind it was something just as spiritual and good as could be asked for.

'Thirdly, I learned how fortunate and what a great obligation to others I had because I was strong, sure, normal, adventuresome, and I was needed. But this posed a serious problem. It posed obligations which I was not ready for, obligations to peoples' feelings. I learned that I, like everyone could hurt people very much if I wasn't careful. I found too that many boys my own age more or less, were fighting being homosexual so hard they were getting all mixed up, some turning to crime to prove themselves men, some giving up and acting like girls, others sinking into their own black pits. I knew that somehow I could help them. The only way I knew was to make friends with as many people as I could find, and let them ask for help; having an affinity for slums I spent a great deal of time in the pool halls and hang-outs. But I needed too the stability of the more affluent and also spent time "up-town". My work went towards photography and the arts for a living, although whatever job came along was exciting, particularly if I'd never tried it before. The war came and I joined the Navy, after my discharge I worked for youth camps and reform schools, but this did not have the same effect as when by accident I would meet someone who really needed me ... Let me also say, that there were more heterosexuals than homosexuals in my life and I never let them know my feelings, not because I was ashamed of them, but many would lose their confidence in me because they wouldn't understand.

'By the early fifties I was thirty and for a long time had thought it was time to do my own thing ... this meant going to school and as I had no high school I decided to go to Europe where I could learn what I wanted without going to high school first and then being obliged to take all the other courses our colleges make one take which are alien to their chosen profession. I saved up four hundred dollars and headed for Europe, spending almost ten years there I found there were many people there needed me as a friend even though I was not a good linguist. Arriving back home in the early sixties I found myself living in the midst of the notorious height ashbury district, I think it was here where I learned the most and the fastest ... For within a few years it turned from a place where searching young people came to find truth to a place where they came to hide from life ... But in the first years I learned a great deal and my age and experience help a lot of others. I had a large apartment and made it a home for those who had none. Thus I met all sorts during that three years period. Now I am fifty and am working in an entirely different world of people, but I think the end results are much the same.

JUSTIN'

CHAPTER FOUR

The Author sat in his office and grinned a grin of great appreciation. It was not an 'office', really, but a most uncomfortable metal bed with no springs. One of those things that went up or down at the touch of a button and then, when the bed was at its highest—the electricity would be cut somewhere. But it was the only office the Author possessed. Now he sat in his office—such as it was—and grinned with sheer pleasure.

Mr. Harold Wilson, the former Prime Minister of England, was reported on the Canadian radio as having 'said his piece' about the Press. His remarks were to the effect that if the Press could get hold of a story, they distorted it. If they could not get hold of the story, they imagined it.

EXACTLY!

That is what the Author had been saying for YEARS—a lone voice crying out in the wilderness. The Press, in the Author's opinion, is FOUL! He always wondered how they got the idea that they were 'special'. A few years ago gossiping people were dunked in the village duck-pond. Now, if a person has a yen for garbage he joins the Press as a reporter. The Author, having bitter experience of the Press, very firmly believed that that gang is the most evil force on the Earth today, responsible for wars and strikes. However, the truth about the Press is not popular with Publishers, so as there is no opposition, that evil weed flourishes unchecked.

The Author sat in his office—the aforementioned bed—and contemplated his surroundings. A scruffy bed-table bought about a hundredth-hand from some local hospital, a beat-up old Japanese typewriter, and an even more beat-up old Author, the latter falling apart at the seams.

About seventy letters littered the bed. Fat Taddy the Siamese, wallowed among them, every so often rolling on

4

her back and kicking her legs in the air. 'Shrimps, shrimps,' she muttered, 'why don't we have shrimps, eh? That's what I want to know!' Beautiful Cleopatra, her sister, sat beside the Author, her arms folded, an enigmatic smile on her face. 'Boss!' she said suddenly, rising and flicking an imagined speck of dust from her tail. 'Boss, why don't you get in the wheelchair and we will go out and watch the ships. Dull in here, eh?'

Just outside the window the Polish liner, the 'Stefan Batory' was getting ready to sail. The Blue Peter, the blue flag with the white square in the centre, had just been hoisted and crowds were gathering as is ever the case when a liner is about to sail. For several moments the Author was tempted. 'Aw, why not?' he thought, then Virtue triumphed again—besides, he had an extra twinge of pain just then—so he remarked, 'No, Clee, we have to work, we have to put some words on paper to pay for those shrimps that Taddy is still groaning about.' Miss Cleo yawned and leaped lightly to the floor and sauntered off. Miss Taddy gave a final roll and kick, and followed.

The Author gave a sigh that almost blew all the letters off his bed and reached for a handful. One letter fell open. 'How is it,' the writer thundered, 'that you DARE to say that you will not answer letters unless money for postage is enclosed? Don't you know that people do you an honour when they spend their money and time in writing to you? You have a DUTY to reply to all letters and give all information asked for!'

'Tut, tut!' thought the Author. 'There is one biddy who is going to get a surprise.' The typewriter was a heavy old thing, knee-cracking when endured for too long, but the Author had no sylph-like figure and although he had slimmed from a modest two hundred and eighty-something pounds, two hundred and fifteen was the rock-bottom limit even on a thousand-calorie a day diet. The problem was, was his bay-window too 'bay' or were his arms too short. Secretary? No sir, no ma'am. No secretary, and only authors who write pornographic stuff make enough to pay a secretary.

So, our Author glumly grabbed the old typewriter and dragged the wretched thing on to his knees. 'Dear Miss Buggsbottom,' the keys clattered, 'your kind letter has been received but not WELL received. May I take the opportunity to "put you straight", or "wise you up", as the Americans say? My mail is going up, Miss Buggsbottom, and so are mail charges. Now, the cost in time and material is now calculated as being MORE than three dollars to send out one single-page letter. Contrary to your assumption, I do NOT get a dollar on each book sold. I receive from seven to ten per cent of the lowest price in the country in which the book is printed.'

The Author snorted and fumed with indignation: 'From this I may have to pay the first publishers fifty per cent—don't ask me why! Then there are other commissions to pay, losses on currency conversion, and TAX. So, Miss Buggsbottom, you really do not know what you are writing about. Ah yes, an author has to EAT as well, you know!'

Ra'ab came in: 'Mail has come,' she said, 'only sixty-three today. Must be held up somewhere.' Reminded the Tattered Author of another letter he had tucked away. He fished in the first pile and came up with a gaudy orange sheet with some quite improbable flowers printed all around the edges. 'Ah!' he said, 'Here it is.' Unfolding it, he read: 'You say you are a monk. How is it, then, that there is a "Mrs."? Some monk, eh? How are you going to explain that?'

The poor Author sighed anew in his exasperation. 'What queer things people are!' he thought, but the answer, typed, might help someone. Ladies and gentlemen: have you ever heard of a nunnery where there has been a priest? Have you ever heard of a community where a man can live with a woman, with women? They are not always doing the things which the prurient think they will be doing. Have you ever heard of a prison (for example) which has a female nurse? Come to that, have you ever heard of a solitary night nurse on a mens' ward? Come! Come! In the better communities men and women are not ALWAYS jumping into bed together. Oh, naughty, naughty. What thoughts people have!

The same Esteemed Correspondent (Esteemed should be reversed!) also went on to write, 'and why do you wear a beard, to hide a funny mouth or something?' But the Great Public would be amazed if they knew the rot which the component parts making up the Great Public wrote. Here is an actual extract—no, the whole letter which was received from one peculiar person. It is absolutely true and unaltered: 'Dear Sir, I must be FREE, free to live my own life without being ordered about by others. I must be FREE or my soul will die. Send me one million dollars by return. (signed . . .) P.S. Thanks in advance.'

The Author, having typed it from the original, turned it over and over in his hands. Some of the letters were . . . FUNNY. He sighed again, probably lack of oxygen from the stale, polluted air of the city, and tossed the letter into the garbage bin. Pfah! 'You can say that again,' muttered Fat Taddy as she sauntered in. But Life and Letters move on. More about homosexuals? What a furor. Some people opposed to them would completely spoil their fun with their sharp knives. But here is something about the distaff side of it.

The underground Bar in the wilder reaches of Soho, London, where ANYTHING goes, was almost empty. A thuggish-looking bar-tender was leaning up against the far wall of his domain, idly picking his teeth and thinking of nothing in particular. At the distal end of the bar two people sat on high stools and muttered low in conversation about low subjects—waist-high subjects.

Lotta Bull was the epitome of the masculine woman, lacking only certain essential attachments to make her a complete man. Her hair was clipped short in almost military fashion, her hard face would have been an asset to a sergeant-major in a tantrum. Her dress was the most unisex of unisex, and her voice was as deep as the voices of the ships in the Pool of London. She cast a proprietorial eye on the girl before her.

Rosie Hipps was all feminine, fluff, and froth with hardly a thought in her vapid blonde head. With the blue eyes and curls of a china doll she gave an impression of demure innocence. Rosie Hipps was curved, as curved as Lotta Bull was straight. Rosie delicately dangled a cigarette in a very long holder; Lotta chewed on the end of one of those small cheroots.

A customer entered the bar and stood for a moment gazing around. Spotting Rosie Hipps he started in her direction, but changed course abruptly in midstream at the sight of Lotta Bull's fierce glare. Discreetly he moved off in the direction of the barkeep now straightened up and polishing glasses. 'Let that doll alone,' whispered the barkeep, 'or her butch will DO ya. She's a WILD one, that Lotta Bull. What'll ya have?'

'Men! That's all they think about!' snorted Lotta. 'I'd kill the man who approached ME the wrong way. Women is MY meat, cleaner. Cleaner. Have YOU ever had a man, Rosie?'

Rosie smiled, then laughed outright at her private thoughts. 'Let's go somewhere,' she said, 'this is no place to talk.' Quickly they emptied their glasses and sauntered out into the street. 'Let's get a taxi,' she said.

A quick flick of her hand, and Lotta Bull had a London taxi turn in its own length in the street and come to a halt beside them. The driver watched them get in, pushed down his fare flag and nodded knowingly as Lotta gave the address in an obscure street in Paddington, just by the backside of the Hospital. Traffic was light—for London—at this time of the evening. Office workers had gone home, shops were closed, and it was yet too early for the cinema and theatre crowds. The taxi sped along, avoiding the lumbering red buses, passing the familiar Green Line vehicles also on their hurried journeys from and to the country beyond the city.

The taxi swung around a corner and came to a gentle halt. Lotta Bull peered at the fare meter and fumbled in her purse before paying. 'Thanks a lot, sir,' said the taxi-driver, 'have a good trip.' With the familiarity of long practice he meshed gears and sped off down the road in search of the next fare.

Lotta Bull stomped stolidly across the sidewalk. Rosie Hipps teetered along after her on heels so high that everything shook and bounced in the right places. Sundry men, of all ages, abroad in the street, did a swivel-head turn and whistled appreciatively, drawing frosty stares from Lotta.

The key grated in the lock and with an almost inaudible 'snick' the door swung open. Lotta fumbled for the light switch, and the entrance room was flooded with light. They entered and the door swung shut behind them. 'Ah!' breathed Rosie Hipps as she sank gratefully into a low chair and pulled off her shoes, 'My feet are killing me!' Lotta swung into the kitchen and plugged in the electric kettle.

'Cuppa char, that's what I want,' she said, 'I'm dry as a bone.'

The tea was hot, the cakes pleasant. Together they sat on the 'Antique from Liberty's' love-seat and with a low table before them. 'You were going to tell me, Rosie, about this first man of yours,' said Lotta, reaching out a foot and pushing away the table. She swung her shoeless feet on to the love-seat and pulled Rosie down beside her.

Rosie laughed and said, 'Quite the damndest thing, really. That was a few years ago. I didn't know the difference between a boy and a girl then. Didn't know there WAS a difference, Mum was VERY strict. So I was going to Sunday School in those days—I was about sixteen I guess. The teacher was a young fellow, maybe twenty years of age. He seemed friendly and I was flattered. Got a nice little Vauxhall car, too, so he must have been well off, I thought.' She stopped to light a cigarette and blew a cloud of smoke into the air.

'Many times after Sunday School he wanted to drive me home, but I always said no as Mum was so strict. So he suggested driving me and dropping me off at the end of our street. I said yes and got in the car. All green it was, very nice car too. Well, he took me home several times and once we stopped in the Park—we lived in Wandsworth then. He seemed to have difficulty with his breathing or something, and I did not know a thing he was talking about and as his hands were so busy I thought he was wanting a fight or something—poor fool that I was. But then a policeman on a horse came round the corner and the fellow just jammed in the gears and we took off like scared rabbits.'

She fiddled with her cigarette and mashed it in the ashtray. For a few moments there was silence, broken at last by Lotta Bull saying, 'Well? What then?'

Rosie Hipps heaved such a sigh that she almost popped over the top and then continued, 'Mum was SUCH a prude. There was no man ever in the house. Dad had been killed in an accident soon after I was born. I had no male relatives at all, no pets—nothing. The "Birds and the Bees" lark was lost on me. Oh sure, at school we girls fooled round together, as girls will. We explored every avenue as the politicians say, but boys—no. There was a bit of talk about them, but the remarks were quite beyond my understanding. I knew there were Christians and I knew there were Jews, and I thought the difference between boys and girls was much about the same, one went to a different church or a different school or something.'

She paused to light a fresh cigarette, coughing quite a bit as she drew breath at the wrong moment. Lotta Bull sat up to pour herself a fresh cup of tea and downed the tepid stuff in one mighty swallow. She lay back and put her arms around Rosie, 'Yes?' she enquired, running her hands up and down as if she was practising the violin.

'Well, how can you expect me to talk when you are doing THAT?' asked Rosie. 'Wait until I've told you, if you want to hear, you want your cake set to music or something?'

Lotta put her arms around Rosie's waist again and said, 'Aw, shucks, you got a dose of the innocents again? Talk!'

'Well,' said Rosie, 'I didn't see him at all until the next Sunday School. He looked a bit scared at me and whispered, "Did you tell your mother?" So of course I told him no, I didn't tell HER everything. He looked relieved and then went on teaching us the Good Word. Then he said that a man from the Band of Hope wanted to talk to us because we should sign the Pledge to be good little teetotallers or something. Didn't mean a thing to me as I had never tasted the stuff.'

Outside there was an almighty crash as two cars collided with a tinny jangle. Lotta Bull jumped up so violently that poor Rosie was tipped over onto the floor. Lotta rushed to the window and peered out at the scene below, pedestrians standing gaping, two drivers shouting indecent imprecations at each other, and then—the Police. 'Fuzz!' gloomed Lotta. 'Never COULD stand the fuzz, they always spoil everything. Come on, Rosie, get with it again.' They resumed their places on the love-seat—so aptly named— and Rosie continued.

'After Sunday School I was going home when HE drove up beside me and opened the car door. I got in and he drove off, we went along to Putney and sat in the car by the side of the river. Of course, there were a lot of people about, so we just sat and talked. He said a lot of things which I just did not understand ... THEN! He said how silly I was to always go by what my mother told me. "Come up to

Maidenhead with me next Saturday," he said, "tell your mother you are going out with a girl-friend. I know a nice little place, we will have FUN." So I said I would think about it and then he drove me home after arranging to meet me after school on Friday.

'Mother was a perfect beast all that week. "What is the matter with you, Rosie?" she kept on. At school everything went wrong. My girl-friend, Milly Coddle, took a sudden hate to me—you know, one of those things that girls get—and life was perfectly miserable. I was one of the prefects, and the Head bawled me out for not reporting various things which I had not even seen. Then when I said I had not seen them, she told me I wasn't fit to be a Prefect; oh, it was a BEASTLY week!'

Poor Rosie stopped and gasped with indignation as all the memories came flooding back. 'Then the Headmistress asked me if I were in trouble or something. I said no, only the trouble she was giving me, and then she turned red and said she would speak to my mother about my saucy manner. Oh Lord! I thought, now I've had EVERYTHING. But the week crawled, I mean CRAWLED.'

Lotta Bull nodded her head in sympathy. 'Let's have a drink, eh Rosie?' she asked, rising and going to the Fitted Bar in the corner of the room. 'What'll you have? Scotch? Gin and Tonic? Vodka?'

'No, I'm common today, give me a Watneys,' said Rosie, 'all my hopes are on the bier now, so give me a beer.'

Together they sat on the love-seat, Lotta with Scotch on the Rocks, and Rosie with her Watneys. 'Gee! You are interesting me,' exclaimed Lotta, 'care to tell me the rest?'

'So, on Friday morning before school,' resumed Rosie, 'Mum got a letter from the Head—the old beast—and as Mum read she turned a horrid purple. "Rosie," Mum yelled as she finished the letter (it must have been a corker!) "Rosie, you just wait until you come back from school. I'll lambast you, I'll take the hide off your back, you ... you ...!" she gasped and spluttered and words failed her. I fled. At school that day I was in trouble from start to finish; everyone was LIVID at me.' She paused to take a drink and to re-collect her thoughts.

'HE was waiting just beyond the school gates. BOY! Was I ever glad to see him! I ran to the car and jumped in. He drove away fast and we parked farther on—you know that little square—and I told him all my troubles. I told him I was afraid to go home. "Tell you what," he said at last, "you write a note to your mother and I will get a boy to deliver it. Say you're spending the night with your girlfriend Molly Coddle." So I tore a page out of my exercise book and scribbled a note.' Lotta nodded her head avidly.

'Soon after HE had got a boy on a bicycle to deliver the note, we were speeding up the road towards Maidenhead. On the outskirts there was a nice little place, you know, cabins. Bit of a restaurant there, too. He booked a room for us and then we went in and had a meal. It was about time, too, for I was absolutely STARVED. Mum had been going on so at me that I, well, I just had to miss my breakfast in order to get away from the racket. I mean, one just can't eat when another person is screaming at one. Then you know what school meals are! School dinners are something to be forgotten if at all possible.' She tossed her head and wrinkled her nose at the mere thought.

'Yes,' muttered Lotta Bull sourly, 'but you should see what they gave us in the Reformatory! But go on.'

'So I was truly famished.' resumed Rosie Hipps. 'I ate everything I could, but HE kept on talking, not that I listened, I was too busy eating. Seemed he wanted to play around. Oh! What's it matter? I thought, only the same thing as Molly Coddle and I do together. What if he is different from me in some strange way? Can't a Christian worship with a Jew? Oh! What an ignorant fool I was!'

She sat back and laughed ruefully at the memory, took a sip of her drink, and resumed her narrative. 'Well, I'd had a lot to eat and a lot to drink—tea, you know, and I looked around for the "Ladies" and could not see it so I said for us to go across to the room. We went across the car-park and into the room we had booked. The bathroom door was standing open, so I said I had to go in. Well, I was rather a long time, what with one thing and another, but at last I was finished in there so I switched off the light and went into the bedroom.' She stopped, with a short, hard laugh. Lotta Bull was sitting there with her mouth slightly open. Taking a drink, she resumed:

'I turned round, and there HE was. My God, I never had such a shock before—there he was naked as the day he was born. But, oh my God! He was all hairy and he had a terrible growth-thing sticking out. "He's got a cancerous growth" I thought to myself, then he moved towards me and I slid to the floor in a dead faint. Must have caught my head against the edge of a chair or something, because I REALLY was knocked out.' Lotta Bull was panting with emotion and her eyes were beginning to look wild.

Rosie Hipps continued, 'After what seemed to be a very long time I was aware of things again. There seemed to be a terrible weight thumping about on me. "Oh my God!" I thought drowsily. "An elephant is sitting on me." I opened my eyes and let out a screech of terror. HE was lying on me, and I was bath-naked too. Gee, he was hurting me. Then you know, the damndest thing, he jumped free of me and flapped down on his knees and started praying hard. Then there was the sound of running feet, a key was jammed in the door, and two men burst in. And all I was covered with was a blush of shame!'

Lotta Bull sat back with her eyes half closed, probably visualising the scene. But Rosie went on, 'One of the men stared at me, everywhere, and said, "Heard ye screech, Miss, was he raping you?" Without another word they both rushed at the Sunday School teacher and kicked him hard in all sorts of places. He just bellowed out prayers. "Better get yer clothes on, Miss," said one of the men, "we will call the cops." "Oh my God," I thought. "What will happen now?" I dashed into my clothes and was frightened to see that I had a lot of blood on my legs, but I had to dress.'

'What happened then, did they get the police?' asked Lotta Bull.

'They sure did!' answered Rosie. 'Better than anything on the telly. A police car rushed up, and then right behind there was some jerk from the Press. He leered at me and licked his chops as he opened his notebook. A policeman stopped him. "Let her go," he said, "she may be under age." So the jerk from the Press did the eyeball ogle at the Sunday School teacher who was standing there like a peeled banana. The men would not let him dress until the police came. By now I understood the difference between a man and a woman!'

Outside a newsboy was crying, 'Speshul! Crime of the

Century! Speshul.'

'That's what they do,' said Lotta Bull, 'the Press get hold of some little incident and make a big thing out of it. But what happened then?'

'Well,' said Rosie Hipps, 'the police asked a lot of questions. My! What a brou-ha-ha there was! They asked me a lot of questions, did I go into the room with him willingly. I said yes, but I did not then know what he wanted. I said I did not know the difference between a man and a woman. They laughed like DRAINS at that and the pressman scribbled feverishly. "I do now," I added, and he scribbled again. Suddenly the Sunday School teacher broke free and dropped to his knees where he babbled out prayers by the bucketful. Then, good heavens, he rose to his feet and accused ME of leading him on! I never felt so humiliated in my life.'

'Did they take you to the police station?' asked Lotta.

'Yes, they did. I was put in the police car beside the driver and the other policeman and the Sunday School teacher got in the back and we drove off to the Maidenhead Police Station. The Press tagged on behind. By now there were seven of them. At the police station I was rushed into a room and a doctor and a woman police officer made me take off all my clothes. They spread my legs apart—my! was I ever embarrassed?—and examined me. The doctor called out about marks, bruises, and all that, and the woman officer wrote it all down. Then the doctor stuck a tube thing up me and told me he was just drawing off a specimen to see if I had been raped. God! What else did he think had happened to me.'

She stopped and picked up the glass which Lotta had just refilled. After a good drink, as if to wash away bad memories, she continued, 'After what seemed to be hours and hours a man and woman police took me home to Mum. Mum was white and stuttering with rage. She waved a paper with great big headlines which said that "Schoolgirl ruins prominent Sunday School teacher". Mum was LIVID, and I mean LIVID. She told the police to take me off anywhere, but she had finished with me—and the door slammed with a crash. The cop and copess looked at each other. The woman took me back to the police car and the man stayed knocking at the door.'

She stopped to light a cigarette and then went on, 'At last

the policeman came back and said that Mum had shut the door on me for ever. He looked at me with some sympathy and said they would' have to take me to a Salvation Army Home for Wayward Girls—me! So, to cut a long story short, I was lodged for the night in the awful old building that YOU know so well.'

Lotta Bull sniffed. 'Sure do!' she remarked acidly. 'That's where I learned about the Birds and Bees and discovered that Pot was not to sit on, but tell me the rest about you.'

Rosie Hipps looked rather pleased at Lotta's sustained interest, and went on with her story. 'That night I learned all about Life. Learned all about sex. Boy-o-boy! Some of those girls were crazy, I mean CRAZY! The things they did to each other. But anyhow even that endless night of Hell passed and in the morning I was given breakfast—which I couldn't eat—and then I was taken off to Court and I DON'T mean Buckingham Palace!' She sat silent for a few moments, collecting her bitter thoughts, then, lighting a fresh cigarette, she resumed her tale.

'The policewoman who came for me treated me as if I were a dangerous criminal. She sure was rough with me. I told her I was the injured one. "Sez you!" she replied. Well, after a very long wait I was pushed into the courtroom— oh! it was AWFUL! The Press were there, Mum sat glowering at me, and they brought the Sunday School teacher and put him in the dock. I had to tell all. Some of the men were panting, when I was asked did I go willingly with him. I said I did but I did not know what he wanted. Everybody guffawed. Oh! I can hardly bear to think about it even now.' She stopped and dabbed at her eyes with a minute scrap of lace.

'But anyway,' she continued, 'they said that I was of the Age of Consent, just over sixteen, and a pressman who had been doing a feature story of our school rushed to babble that he had seen me run to the car and jump in. There was no force used, he said. So they let off the Sunday School teacher with a warning to be a good boy in the future. My! He sure did beat it out of that Court!' She stopped and stubbed out her cigarette and took a drink.

'Then they started on me,' she said. 'I was a bad, ungrateful, wicked girl. Even my poor long-suffering widowed mother who had been working her fingers to the bone for me for sixteen years had got sickened by me and had turned me out, rejected me, and wanted nothing more to do with me. So the Court had to do something about it to save my soul. Then a Probation Officer or something clattered to her hind legs and said her piece. The old boy trying the cases fiddled with his glasses, consulted a book or two and then said I would have to go to a School for Wayward Girls for two years.'

Lotta Bull nodded in mute sympathy. Rosie continued, 'Well, that just broke me up. I mean, I hadn't done ANY-THING. So I told them what happened just as calmly as I could as I wanted to make the record clear. The old boy said I was a very rude girl and most ungrateful. "Next case," he called, and I was hustled away to a cell. Some old geezer thrust a sandwich in my shaking hand and someone else pushed a great thick mug of cold tea at me. Of course I couldn't touch the stuff.'

'Just like when they got me,' said Lotta Bull, 'but go on.'

Rosie drew a deep breath and said, 'Then some woman came in and told me that I could not go to the school today and I should have to spend the night in Holloway Prison. Just imagine, me in Holloway, and I really hadn't done a thing. But they took me there in a Black Maria. It was AWFUL. I've never felt so alone in my life.' She stopped and shuddered, and then said, simply, 'And that's how it was with me.'

Lotta Bull moved a cushion and a book fell to the floor with a soft plop. She moved a long arm and picked it up. Rosie looked at the cover and smiled with interest, 'Quite a good book,' said Lotta, 'wait a moment,' she fumbled at the pages, 'read this, he writes quite a bit about homos and lesbians. You should read it. I agree with every word of it.'

Rosie Hipps laughed with considerable affection. 'Read it?' she said. 'I have all the books he has written and I know every one to be true. I write to him, you know.'

Lotta Bull laughed. 'Aw, go on!' she said. 'He's the hermitest hermit of them all. How could you know him?'

Rosie smiled a secret smile and said, 'He helped me a lot. He helped me when I thought I was going mad. That's how I know him!' She fished in her handbag and eventually produced a letter. 'This is from him,' she said as she passed it to Lotta.

Lotta read and nodded her approval. 'What is he really like?' she asked.

'Oh, a bit of a square,' answered Rosie. 'Like, he doesn't drink or smoke. Women are just abstract concepts to him. Just as well too,' she added, 'because he has the sex appeal of last week's cold rice pudding. No, he thinks that if women stayed at home and looked after the kids the world would be a better place. You know, no junkies, no punks.'

Lotta Bull frowned in concentration. 'No women, eh? Is he ... ONE OF US—homo?'

Rosie Hipps sat back and laughed until the tears came to her eyes. 'Good gracious, NO!' she exclaimed. 'You've got him all wrong. Anyhow,' she said sadly, 'the poor guy is stuck now between his bed and his wheelchair.'

'Gee, I'd like to meet him!' breathed Lotta.

'Not a hope!' replied Rosie. 'He doesn't meet people any more. He has had some foul Press creeps cook up an absolute swatch of lies about him and misrepresent everything he has said or done. Now he thinks the Press is the most evil force on this world. I know the Press was the cause of ME going to the Corrective School,' she added reflectively.

'Aw well,' said Lotta Bull, rising to her feet, 'guess we should be going down to the Expresso.'

62

CHAPTER FIVE

The gentle rain came drifting down as though wafted earthwards by a compassionate Goddess of Mercy bringing renascent life to an arid area. The softly falling water, as tenuous as a mist, hesitated and wavered as though uncertain of its destination, then, touching the dry soil, there was a faint hiss and the moisture vanished into the depths. In the soil little rootlets stirred to a dim awareness at the liquid touch, stirred to awareness, and avidly absorbed the life-giving water. As though by the waving of a miracle wand, the first tiny specks of green appeared on the surface of the land. A faint dusting of green which grew and thickened as the rain increased.

Now the rain had increased to a torrential downpour. Huge drops fell and raised small gouts of earth, besmirching the newly-green plants with sodden mud. Here and there the first tiny buds appeared. In this desolate region Nature was prepared to move fast, to put forth vegetation at the first sign of moisture. Small insects scurried busily from plant to plant and leaped from pebble to pebble.

From a nearby depression in the ground there came a faint, strange hiss, followed by gurglings and the tinkle of rolling stones. Soon there came the first swelling waters of a rivulet, carrying a scum of un-wetted soil, drowned insects, and the dry debris of an area a long time without water.

The clouds lowered even more. The monsoon weather of India butted against the Himalayas and spilled torrents of water from upset, heavily-laden clouds. Lightning flashed and the thunder roared and re-echoed against the mountain sides. Here and there lightning struck viciously against a towering pinnacle, shattering it, exploding it into a cloud of dust and stones which came tumbling down the steep mountainsides to thud heavily against the sodden earth below. A boulder toppled and fell with a soggy splash into a pool of water, crushing plants, spewing mud all over the rocks.

The river, in full spate, overflowed its banks and the tributaries found their flow reversed. The willows found the waters climbing higher up their trunks. Birds cowered forlornly in the topmost branches, too wet to fly and fearing the end of the world. The rain fell. The marshes became lakes. The lakes became inland seas. Thunder boomed and roared around the valleys, with the endless, senseless echoes a thousand times repeated, making a mind-stunning medley of sound.

The day darkened and became as the dark of a moonless night. The rain fell as though in solid sheets. No longer was there a discernible river-course, now the whole land seemed covered with turbulent water. A howling gale sprang up and lashed the surface of the flood into white froth. The shriek of the wind rose higher and became a shrill keening which tore at the nerves and gave one thoughts of souls in torment. There came a vivid flash as though the sun were exploding, and a shattering crash of thunder, and the rain stopped as though upon the turning off of a tap. A shaft of sunlight pierced through the darkness, was momentarily obscured, and then the clouds were overcome and rolled back to let the light of day shine again upon the flooded world.

Dotted around, on the higher ground where there was yet some semblance of firmness, dark grey masses of boulder-like proportions suddenly hove to sturdy feet and became monolithic yaks with sodden hair streaming rivulets of water from broad backs. Lethargically they shook themselves, sending sprays of water all around them. Satisfied that they were rid of all running water, they nuzzled the drier ground in the endless quest for food.

Beneath the precarious shelter of a mighty rock outcrop came excited chattering. Gradually figures emerged, muttering imprecations against the inclement weather. Groaning, they stripped off their sopping clothing and wrung it dry and donned it again. Soon, from humans and animals, a faint haze of steam rose as they dried out in the increasing heat of the day.

A young man detached himself from the group and went running across the land, skipping from dry patch to dry patch as best he could. At his heels a huge mastiff barked and gambolled. With shouts and barks the pair set the yaks moving in the direction of the others and then, that accomplished, man and mastiff set out to round up the ponies clustered against a distant rock wall.

A rough path led between fallen rocks to a space which had been cleared at the foot of the mountain, from thence the path deviated and wound upwards for some three hundred feet, terminating in a rock shelf upon which grew a straggly bush some six feet high. Beyond the bush the rockface gave way to an opening, the entrance to a rather large cave eventually leading to tunnels from a long-extinct volcano.

A speck of colour, no, two specks of colour, showed to the careful observer. At the mouth of the cave sat a Lama and his acolyte, both dry and at ease, both looking out over the vast Plain of Lhasa, observing the rapid run-off of the waters hitherto flooding the land. The unexpected cloudburst had left the air even clearer than usual and the pair gazed out over the familiar landscape.

From far away the golden roof-tops of the Potala shot out blinding gleams of light as the sun was reflected from the many facets and angles. The newly-painted front of the building gleamed with ochre and Prayer Flags whipped and weaved in the stiff breeze. The buildings of the Medical School on Iron Mountain looked strangely fresh and clean, and the buildings of the village of Shö glittered brightly.

The Serpent Temple and Lake were clearly to be seen, and the willows in the water were nodding their heads as if in some unspoken agreement. Faint dots of colour showed that monks and Lamas were going about their everyday business. A thin thread of pilgrims could be discerned making their way along the Inner Road of the Pilgrims' Circuit on their Act of Faith journey from the Cathedral of Lhasa to the Potala and back. The Western Gate was shining in the sunlight, and a straggle of traders could be seen passing between the Pargo Kaling and the small nunnery opposite.

Below, at the foot of the mountain, the traders had succeeded in loading their yaks and mounting their ponies. Now, with many a shout and jest, they were making their slow way along to the pass leading down, down, into the lowlands of Tibet and China.

5

Slowly the lowing of the yaks, the barking of the dogs, and the shouts of the humans, passed out of hearing, and peace and silence descended once again.

The Lama and the acolyte surveyed the scene before them. In the distance, to the left of Chakpori, the ferryman could be seen in his inflated hide boat. Frantically he stabbed downwards with his long pole, trying to reach river bottom and stop from being washed away on the swollen crest of the overflowing river. Desperately he reached out and probed deeply down. His boat tipped beneath him, gave a sideways shimmy and slid away, leaving the boat-man struggling and drowning in the flood waters. The boat sped on, lighter now, and borne by the swift waters and sped faster by the breeze. The long pole drifted idly in the shallows which had ironically been so near, while the boatman floated face-down after them.

High overhead the vultures swooped and wheeled in their search for food, staring with keen eyes towards any human or creature in distress. One tentatively dived on the drowned boatman and swerved away at the last moment, observing closely. Seeing no motion the bird swooped again and landed on the dead man's back. Preening itself a moment, the bird looked round defiantly, and then went to work on the back of the man's head.

'Tomorrow,' said the Lama to the acolyte, 'we will travel down to the lower reaches and call upon our friends. For this day we will rest and relax, and it will be an opportunity for us to conserve our energies. The journey will be long and arduous. I see there are a few sticks washed by the base of those rocks.' He rose to his feet and pointed. 'So you go and collect them and we will prepare tea and tsampa.' He smiled slightly, and remarked, 'And after that I will give you some basic instruction in relaxation and in breathing. Both matters in which you are notoriously deficient. For the nonce, collect the wood.' He turned and entered the cave.

The small acolyte scrambled to his feet and reached for a length of rope set to one side. Coiling it around his waist and over his shoulder and so placing himself in grave jeopardy of hanging, he shuffled off down the path to the floor of the valley. About to round a large boulder, he checked himself suddenly. THERE was a large bird sitting preening itself and drying out feathers be-sodden by the recent downpour.

The small acolyte stopped and pondered upon his course of action; IF he waited until the bird buried its head beneath a wing he could steal forward and give it a bump up the behind—to its great amazement! But if he wriggled forward on his stomach, he could grab the bird by the foot. The first idea was obviously the best. He edged forward, holding his breath—inching forward until he was pressed flat against the side of the boulder.

The bird scratched, preened its feathers and flapped its wings. Then, satisfied that it could be no cleaner, it settled comfortably on the rock and buried its head beneath a wing. Entranced, the small boy hurried forward, stumbled over a fallen stone and fell headlong. The bird, roused so suddenly by the fright, reacted as birds will; it ejected a noxious 'gift' over the small acolyte's face and then lumbered heavily into the air. The small boy fumbled desperately at eyes which were suddenly glued shut. From the cave-mouth above there came a soft chuckle.

At last the acolyte clawed the sticky, smelly mass from his face and eyes and made for a small pool of water set in a hollow of the rocks. There, very reluctantly, he dipped his face in the ice-cold water and scrubbed himself fairly clean. From above came the exhortation: 'Don't forget the wood!' The boy jumped, he had forgotten all about it. Turning, he made off down the rock-strewn path, but temptation was ever in lurk for small boys.

On a great flat rock there swayed an immense boulder. By some freak of nature it had fallen in such a position that it balanced exactly. Now it was teetering forwards and backwards. The young acolyte beamed and moved forward. Placing his hands against one surface he pushed hard, relaxed as the rock swung back, pushed hard again, and gradually built up a greater and greater swing. At last the rock swung far beyond its centre of gravity and toppled with an earth-shaking crash. The boy grinned with satisfaction and turned back towards the cave.

Half-way there he jumped with fright as he received a stern telepathic message which almost cracked his skull. 'Wood,' commanded the message, 'wood! WOOD!' Turning on his heel, he went running down the path again with

'WOOD—WOOD!' drumming through his mind.

At last a large amount of wood was gathered. The young acolyte bundled it together and then passed the end of the rope around the whole pile. The other end of the rope he put around his waist and, dragging and straining, he managed to convey the whole bundle to the mouth of the cave. There the Lama was waiting somewhat impatiently, and he helped break up the wood into suitable sticks for the fire which was speedily kindled.

'Your posture is deplorable,' said the Lama, 'and we shall have to do something about it or you will end up like these Western people whom I have seen when visiting India. Before we start our breathing exercises let me instruct you on an exercise which is most applicable to the present occasion.' He smiled as he told the young boy to rise to his feet.

'This is an exercise which is wonderfully invigorating for those who sit a lot—and you are sitting most of the time,' he said. 'This exercise is very good for reducing abdominal fat. It has the interesting name of "the wood-chopping exercise" because its action simulates the benefit to be obtained when chopping wood. Now, stand up!' He made sure the boy was standing erect. 'Imagine you are chopping wood, imagine you have a very heavy axe in your hands, one of those very, very good axes which have just been brought by traders from Darjeeling. Now, stand firmly, stand very firmly, and have your feet wide apart. Then you must clasp your hands together just as if you were holding the shaft of a heavy axe. Imagine that the head of the axe is on the ground, so take a deep breath and raise your hands and the imaginary axe high above your head until your body has gone to the other extreme and no longer is bending forward but is bending backwards.

'You have to bear in mind that you are lifting a very heavy axe, so let your muscles simulate that—you are lifting a very heavy axe. Then with this heavy axe high above your head hold your breath a moment, then vigorously breathe through the mouth and swing down with the imaginary axe in a very strong motion as if you were cutting a big, big tree trunk. You will not, of course, come to a stop with the impact of the wood and the axe, so instead let your arms swing right down between your legs, let your arms swing down so that your hands are in a line with your feet. You must keep your arms straight, and you must keep your spine straight. You should repeat this exercise several times—now go to it, my boy, and do it with vigour, with at least as much vigour as you used to topple that rock.'

The young boy went through the exercise until at last he stood panting and grunting with the effort. 'Oh, Holy Lama!' he said breathlessly. 'Surely exercises like this could kill a person unless they were in good health. I feel almost faint myself!'

'My dear boy!' said the Lama in some exasperation. 'An exercise like this can do only good except in the case of a person who has a weak heart or except for women who have some feminine ailment. I doubt if your heart is at all defective, but from the way in which you grunt and groan you might well be an old woman and so will have outgrown the female disorders to which I refer. So—try your exercises again.'

The young boy slumped down, sitting hunched up on the ground, fingering his feet. The Lama, who had been standing on the edge of the rock wall looking out across the Valley of Lhasa, turned suddenly and said, 'Why are you so hunched up? Are you ill? Are you suffering pain?'

The young acolyte looked blank for a moment and then replied, 'Ill? Who? Me ill? Me?'

The Lama snorted and went towards the boy replying, 'Yes, ill! You! You are sitting there like an old crone suffering from bunions or corns. You are sitting there like an old crone by the side of the market-place listening to the gossiping of the traders. Are your feet troubling you?' He dropped to his knees and looked at the boy's feet, and then, satisfied that there was nothing wrong, he rose to his feet again. 'Boy, on your feet!' he commanded. 'Here is how to relax your feet. I suppose you got them tired by frightening that poor bird, and then by upsetting a rock which was certainly causing no harm to you. So now you have tired your feet, I will show you how they may be relaxed.'

He took the boy by the shoulders and saw that he was standing upright. 'Now,' he said, 'this will give you better circulation of blood. You must stand on one foot, stand on your left foot first. Then lift your right foot off the ground and shake it from the ankle down, not the whole of the leg, remember, we are dealing with your feet. Shake it. Keep your leg still and violently shake your foot from the ankle down. Shake it for three minutes until it begins to tingle. Then put that foot back on the ground and raise the other leg, and shake that foot for three minutes. Do this three times. It will help you when you have cold feet. It will help you after you have had a long march or when you have been standing too long. It will help you when you have been toppling teetering rocks.' He smiled for a moment, and then said, 'Always do exercises barefooted. Never wear your sandals when doing exercises. There is much benefit to be gained by having one's feet actually in contact with the ground.'

The poor boy groaned and exclaimed, 'Oh, Holy Lama, I feel much more tired now standing up like this, and doing all these exercises has caused my body to ache with tiredness. Can I not rest a while?'

The Lama gave a secret smile, and said, 'You really step into little traps, do you not? You have got yourself tired by doing the things which you should not do, so if I show you the things which you should do, you can avoid getting tired when doing the things you should not do. So let us remove the tiredness from the upper part of your body by the very elementary exercise which our Chinese friends call "Relaxing the Trunk".'

'But, Holy Lama,' said the young acolyte in some dismay, 'I thought we were going to do breathing exercises, not this awful stuff.'

The Lama shook his head reprovingly, and said, 'Boy, these exercises are just the prelude to breathing exercises. Now, pay great attention to me because this particular exercise would better be known as a series of four exercises. It is designed to help your neck, then your shoulders, then the centre of your back, and finally the whole of your body from where your legs join your body to where your head joins your neck.

'First you will stand like this——' He bent down and pushed the boy's feet apart about twenty-four inches. 'Always stand with your feet slightly apart and let your head drop forward as if you have lost the power of the muscles. With your head drooping loosely, let it slowly circle clockwise just once. Your arms will be hanging loose.

After this you will let your head hang lifelessly forward again, but this time you will let your shoulders droop as if you have no muscles. You head is hanging loose, your shoulders are drooping, and your arms are hanging loosely as well. Then, let your shoulders make a clockwise movement, but the head and the arms will remain limp without moving. After you have done this, do it anti-clockwise.'

The poor wretched boy, looking a picture of woebegone misery, went through the exercises. By the time he had finished he did indeed feel lifeless, but the Lama soon snapped him to attention saying, 'Now drop your chest forward and let the whole of the top part of your body make this circular movement. You have to rotate the whole of the top of your body, everything above the waist. After you have done it in one direction, do it in the opposite direction.'

The boy stood there with his feet slightly apart and looking so limp that he appeared in danger of falling over on his face. First his head and shoulders rotated in one direction, then slowly in the other.

'Now,' said the Lama, 'you will have to put your feet slightly farther apart so that you have a very firm stance, then you make everything above the waist absolutely limp and then, bending from the waist, you make a wide circle, as wide as you can possibly manage it without falling over. You make a wide circle clockwise so that you are in some danger of being over-balanced. Continue making these circles, getting smaller and smaller circles until for a moment you are motionless. Then start moving again in the opposite direction making the circles larger and larger until once again you are in danger of overbalancing. Then, when you have done that do it once more, and after that let just your shoulders rotate and counter-rotate. When you have done that once, let your head rotate and counter-rotate. Now!' he said. 'Do you not truthfully feel a lot better?'

The young acolyte looked cautiously at the Lama and said, 'Holy Lama, yes. I must admit I do feel a lot better for that, but I am sure that I would feel even better if I could have a rest after it because, as you said, we have a long and hard journey before us tomorrow, and I fear that these exercises might tire me unduly.'

The Lama laughed and said, 'Well, on this occasion we

will do no more, but throughout our journey down into the lowlands you will have to learn other exercises, you will have to learn about breathing, for our journeys are more than just covering land; we have to cover knowledge as well. The more you learn now the less you have to learn later, until you get to the point of knowing that the more you know the more there is to know. But—be off with you for now.'

So the young acolyte suddenly recovered all his energy and sped down the path in search of any adventure which might present itself. The Lama resumed his seat at the edge of the cliff, and remained gazing out across the beloved Valley of Lhasa where even now the sun was beginning to set, and the lengthening shadows crept across the rock encompassed land.

The shadows turned deeper purple and sped ever faster across the dark floor of the Valley. The western wall of the mountain range already was black with here and there a vague pin-point of light showing as the faintest of flickers. Light shot in golden shards from the Potala, Home of the Inmost One. Behind Iron Mountain the Happy River glinted as a lighter path in a dark abyss.

But swiftly the sun withdrew behind the mountains and the dark of the night seemed to rise up as the waters rise up in times of flood. The eastern wall of the mountain sank deeper and deeper into the approaching night. Soon there was naught but the purple night with the gentle breeze wafting to even this distance a suspicion of incense and rancid butter.

Thousands of feet above the topmost ranges caught a last glimpse of the sun. A golden line like a flaming banner ran along the topmost edge, lingering longer at the highest points, until even they were extinguished in the universal darkness. Time wore on. The people of the night set about their business. A night-bird called and at long last was answered from afar. A lonely mouse squeaked, followed by a scuffle and a shriek abruptly ended.

The night wore on. The stars shone forth in all their hard brilliance in the cold clear air. Bright in the colours never seen from lower lands, they seemed to wink and twinkle as though engaged in some mysterious business far beyond the ken of mortals. Slowly a ghostly silver radiance misted the far horizon, and majestically there lofted into view the gibbous moon with mountains and craters plain for even the unaided eye to see.

Softly the luminescence spilled over into the Valley, shining on frost-whitened peaks, sending brilliant showers of incandescence from the Potala roof-tops. The Happy River turned to molten silver and the waters of the willow lake became as a perfect mirror. The moonlight grew, casting in stark relief the shadow of the Lama sitting motionless by the bush at the edge of the cliff. A probing finger of light wandered into the mouth of the cave to reveal the prone body of the young acolyte sleeping the sleep enjoyed only by small boys.

From a great distance came the rushing rumble of a sudden rock fall, followed after an interval by the crumping thud as mighty boulders struck the earth after tens of thousands of years in one spot. Came too the frightened squawking of some bird which suddenly found cause for alarm in the earth-shake.

The night wore on. Majestically the moon sailed across the sky and withdrew demurely behind the sheltering mountain range. Timidly the stars faded in the approaching light of a new day. The sky became suffused with colour. Bands of light raced from horizon to horizon, growing ever brighter. Night birds croaked sleepily and sought their daytime haunts in secure crevices in the mountainside. The creatures of the night prepared to sleep through another day.

The night wind slowed; for an appreciable space of time there was dead calm, then a slight breeze sprang up in the opposite direction and the creatures of the day bestirred themselves. The small acolyte sat up suddenly, rubbed his eyes, and rushed outside. A fresh day had begun.

It was a simple matter to break the fast of the night. Breakfast, lunch, tea, dinner, call the meals what you will, among the priests of Tibet they were all the same. Tea and tsampa. The roughest, crudest tea of all made specially into bricks, from China. And tsampa—well, there was no other food. These foods, tea and tsampa, provide all that is necessary for the maintenance of health and life.

Breakfast was soon over. The Lama turned to the acolyte and said, 'And what is our next task?'

The acolyte looked hopefully down the sides of his nose and said, 'Should we not have a rest, Honourable Lama? I know where there is a vulture's nest with eggs in. Shall we watch them?'

The Lama sighed and replied, 'No, we have to think of those who will come after us. We must clean the cave, we must see that it is strewn with fresh sand, we must see that it is well stocked with wood, for the next travellers here may be in dire need of fire, of warmth. We have to remember, we should have welcomed wood, so let us do what we would have welcomed.'

The boy went out and moved again down the steeply inclined path, kicking idly at stones as he jogged along—until he kicked at one stone which was not loose but which was bedded deep in the earth. For some minutes he hopped round on one leg uttering strange cries and holding the injured foot between his two hands. But something attracted his attention, a feather came fluttering down from the sky. In the excitement of seeing this large vulture's feather he forgot all about his foot and chased after the falling fragment. It was just a dirty old thing blown along by the wind, so he threw it away and continued his interrupted journey in search of wood.

At last the cave was swept clean with dry sticks, and the inner wall was stacked with wood ready for the next traveller. Then, sitting together on the edge of the rock, the Lama said, 'You will have to learn about breathing. Your breath is noisy like the creaking of a vulture's wings in a breeze. Now, how are you going to sit for your breathing exercises?'

The young acolyte immediately jerked to attention and quickly sat in a most exaggerated Lotus Position. He put his hands palms up in his lap, and on his face appeared an absolutely wooden, frozen expression, while he did some peculiar thing with his eyes as if he was trying to gaze at some imaginary spot a few inches above and in front of him.

The Lama laughed outright, and said, 'No, no, you do not sit like that at all. Breathing is a natural thing. You sit or stand in any way convenient and comfortable. Too many people suffer from a form of dementia when they think of breathing exercises. They think they have to adopt the most extraordinary and unnatural poses, they think that breathing cannot be beneficial unless it is also a considerable hardship. My boy,' he said, 'sit or stand in any way comfortable for you. You can sit straight up, but you must—and this is the only important matter—you must keep your spine as erect as is comfortably possible. The easiest way is to imagine that your spine is a post stuck in the ground and the rest of you is just draped loosely around it. Keep your spine straight then you will not be tired.'

The Lama was already sitting erect with his hands clasped in his lap. He looked at the young acolyte, saying, 'Relax, relax, you must relax. You are not undergoing torture, you are not being a model for one of our butter figures. You are learning to breathe. Just relax, let yourself sit naturally with your spine erect.'

He nodded his approval as the boy sat in an easier manner. Then he said, 'Ah, that's better, that's much better. Now you must breathe in slowly. Let the air fill the lower part of your lungs just as the darkness of the approaching night first fills the lower part of our Valley. Then, let the air rise to fill the middle and the upper part of your lungs. You can actually feel it. But do it without a jerk.' He paused and smiled, and then continued:

'When the shadows of the night herald the passing of the day, first the shadows creep across the ground, then the darkness rises, constantly, smoothly, evenly, without change of speed, without jerk. So it is that you must breathe. As the shadows rise up and darkness fills our Valley at night, so must the air within you rise up and fill your lungs. But as the air enters your lungs, force out your ribs, pretend that the day is hot and your robes are sticking to you. Pull out your robes from your sides. Well, make your ribs come out like that, and you will find that you can take in more and more air.'

He watched to see that the boy was following instructions exactly, and then satisfied that this was so, he continued, 'You can feel your heart thumping, so in this first case let the air flow within you for four good heart beats. You will find that your body expands during the in-breathing period, and shrinks when you breathe out. You should exaggerate slightly the natural expansion and contraction.'

The Lama suddenly spoke sharply, 'No, no, boy! Definitely no! You must keep your mouth shut while you are doing this breathing. Are you trying to catch a fly or something?'

The boy shut his mouth with an audible snap, and the Lama continued, 'The whole purpose of this exercise is to draw air in through your nostrils and to circulate in the air spaces of your body, and then you breathe out again through your nostrils. When I want you to breathe through your mouth, then I will tell you so. But first of all, until you are more proficient at this, you must practise for about fifteen minutes, rising later to about thirty minutes.'

The boy sat and breathed, and the Lama gently raised a hand to serve as an indicator of the correct rate of breathing for the young acolyte.

At last he said, 'Well, that is enough for now. We must set about our business.'

He rose to his feet and dusted the grains of sand from his robe. The boy rose to his feet and copied the Lama's action. Together they looked in the cave to make sure that nothing had been forgotten. Together they went down the path to the floor of the Valley. At the bottom the Lama arranged certain stones to show the way to the cave above. Then turning to the boy he said, 'Go and collect the ponies.'

Gloomily the acolyte moved away looking for any sign of the small horses. At last, climbing on a big rock, he saw them about a quarter of a mile distant. Carefully he manoeuvred from rock to rock until he was within feet of the horses.

The horses looked at each other, and then they looked at the young acolyte. As he walked towards them they walked away at exactly the same speed. The boy changed direction and tried to run ahead. The two horses imperturbedly moved a little faster and maintained the exact distance. By now the boy was getting rather hot and was panting. The horses—the boy was sure of this—each had a cynical sneer on their face.

At last the young acolyte had had enough. He went back to where the Lama was still standing, 'Oh, Honourable Lama,' he said in some frustrated irritation, 'these horses will not let me catch them. They are making fun of me.'

The Lama looked at the poor boy and an amused smile

76

hovered at the corners of his mouth. 'Is that so?' he enquired mildly. 'Then let us see if they will come for me.'

He moved into the open and clapped his hands together. The two ponies had resumed their grazing, but they raised their heads with ears very erect. The Lama clapped his hands again and called for the horses to come. They looked at each other, they looked back at the Lama. They looked at each other again, and both began to trot towards the Lama. He moved to them and patted them, and put his own pack on the back of the larger of the two ponies.

The smaller pony looked at the small acolyte and moved away as the boy approached. At last the boy was running to catch the horse, and the horse was just moving in a circle. The Lama, tiring of the sport, spoke sharply to the pony which immediately stopped and became docile. The boy moved forward, being very very careful to stay clear of the hoof-end, and placed his bundle on the horse's neck.

The Lama nodded and mounted the horse, and sat quiet. The boy took a fantastically big leap to catch the horse unawares, but the horse moved slightly and the boy sailed straight over its back to land with a crash in the sand.

The Lama moved forward with a sigh of resignation saying, 'Oh dear, oh dear. Our daily entertainment—but we are in a hurry.' He leaned down, picked up the small boy, and dumped him unceremoniously on the back of the small pony. 'Come along!' he commanded. 'We have wasted enough time. We have to move or we shall have lost another day.'

Together the horses stepped out across the earth floor, avoiding rocks. The Lama was slightly in the lead. The boy strove to keep up behind. He never was proficient at horse riding, and never would be, but he did his best.

On they rode, the Lama sitting comfortably erect, untired, untroubled. The boy on the smaller pony was sagging like a sack of barley, but, unlike the sack of barley, the boy was getting sorer by the minute. At last, after some three or four hours of travel, the Lama stopped and said, 'We will rest here a while. You may dismount.'

The small acolyte simply ceased to cling to the horse's mane, and slid to the ground in an undignified heap. The horse moved sideways several feet.

CHAPTER SIX

At the edge of the Valley of Lhasa, where the beaten track dips deeply downwards on the way to the sweltering lowlands, and eventually to China, the Lama and the small acolyte rested upon the hard-packed earth. A few yards away the hobbled horses wandered in search of sparse grass. High overhead a large bird wheeled in lazy circles. The small boy watched it half-interestedly; his REAL interest was in the aches and pains which he endured whenever he sat upon a horse. Now he was reclining face down, turning his head sideways from time to time to watch the soaring bird. Soon he drowsed and then slept.

People were resting in other parts of the world too. In a radio factory in the western part of the world workers were having one of their innumerable 'breaks' from the monotony of factory existence. Rusty Nales, the shop carpenter, suddenly hooted with laughter and flung a blue-covered paper-back contemptuously to the floor. 'The guy must be NUTS!' he shouted. 'Gawd! What a lot of rubbish people get away with in books.'

'What's with you, Man?' mildly enquired the dark little Jew, Isadore Shutt, as he stooped and picked up the offending book. Rusty Nales spat his contempt and wiped his mouth on the back of his hand. 'Ahhh!' he exclaimed. 'The whole thing is just plain silly.'

Ivan Austin, the truck driver, grabbed the book from Isadore Shutt and looked at it, ' "Feeding the Flame" by Lobsang Rampa, Oh—HIM!' he exclaimed in disgust. 'Don't believe HIM, do you?' he enquired of no one in particular, continuing. 'The fellow is a NUT, that's what he is—a NUT!'

Shirley May, the telephone girl, bristled with anger. 'That's what YOU think!' she said angrily. 'You haven't the brains to know any better, Bigmouth!' She shrugged her shoulders and glared angrily at poor Ivan Austin.

'Aw, gee, you dumb broad,' he shouted in exasperation, 'even you don't believe that, that'—he fumbled for a word —'that CRAP, do you, why the fellow is a——!'

The door opened and one of the typists, Candy Hayter, wiggled in. 'You folks sure are shouting,' she remarked, 'but I know the truth of these books. That author was accused, tried, and condemned by the putrid Press without having been given ANY chance to defend himself. That's the Press for you, and saps like you'—she glared at poor Rusty Nales and Ivan Austin—'are so stupid that you believe the newspapers hook, line, and sinker. Pah!'

'Yeah, ma'am, that's O.K.,' interjected Bill Collector from the Accounts Department, 'but just you listen to what this crazy guy writes.' He fumbled at the book, polished his glasses and glanced round at his audience before reading: '"Feeding the Flame" by Lobsang Rampa, page 23. Last paragraph. "It is absolutely possible to make a device which will enable one to telephone the astral world. It has actually been done..."' His voice trailed off and there was a moment's silence, broken by Ivan Austin saying, 'See what I mean? It's CRAZY—the guy must have been high on drugs when he wrote that.'

Ernest Truman, Chief of the Research Department, pursed his lips. Then he rose to his feet and went into his office, returning seconds later with a magazine opened at a certain page. 'Now I will enter the discussion,' he said. 'Listen to me while I read extracts from a most influential British magazine.' He stopped, and scanned the page before him. The door opened again and the Works Manager, R. U. Crisp, walked in.

'What gives?' he asked brusquely. 'You people think I'm paying for a Mothers' Meeting? Get moving, get cracking, get back to work! Quick—vamoose—FAST!'

'Mr. Crisp, sir!' said Ernest Truman. 'A minute, sir, in the interest of the advancement of technical knowledge with which we may later be involved, I would like to read these people AND YOU a few paragraphs.'

R. U. Crisp pondered a second and then came to a crisp decision. 'O.K.,' he said. 'I know how earnest is your desire to educate us all, so call in my secretary, Alice May Cling, and she will take a verbatim report on it.' Secretary Cling

79

hurried in together with the canteen girl, Sherry Wines. There was rapt attention as Ernest Truman began to speak. After all, they were getting PAID to listen to this and it was much easier than assembling radios.

'There has been denigration and doubt against the Author Rampa for daring to suggest what is in fact a scientific possibility,' pontificated Ernest Truman. 'He has been the subject of much scoffing for his suggestions and definite statements. Now'—he rustled the magazine—'now, the pre-eminent British Radio magazine the "Wireless World" dated June 1971 has an article on page 312 of that issue under the title of "Electronic Communication with the Dead?" I will read you extracts but you may refer to the publication itself if you wish to read the extensive article concerned.' He stopped, peered over his glasses, wiped his nose, and cleared his throat. Then he read on:

'Free Grid's comments on metamorphosed ψ waves (see page 212, April issue) reminded me of a curious incident which happened to me some years ago and for which I have never been able to find a rational explanation. When I was about fourteen years old I discovered, lying in a loft, an ancient radio of the type which I believe was known in the 1920's as a "det-2 l.f."

'I refurbished this museum piece and, being curious as to its DX capabilities, it became my practice during school holidays to set the alarm for 2 a.m. and to search, using headphones, for American stations.

'But now we come to the curious bit. On two or three occasions over several weeks, at times when I had removed the aerial plug-in coil to change wavelength (which meant that the aerial was virtually open-circuited) a raucous voice burst the silence with a few words; it was clearly speech but so distorted as to be unidentifiable as to content. Only a few words occurred at a time, although I remember waiting for about an hour hoping to hear more, but without success. Most of the European stations had long since closed down and I was remote from any high-power commercial transmitters, neither were any amateurs operating in the area.

'I'd all but forgotten about it until reminded by Free Grid's hypothesis. Then, in the curious way things happen, I came across a newly-published book called "Breakthrough" which I strongly commend to your attention. The author claims that an ordinary common-or-garden tape recorder, if switched on and left to its own devices can, on playback, be found to reproduce voices originating from the dead.

'Now there are few words which are more emotive than "spiritualism", with vehement pro- and anti-camps arising at the mere mention of it. So if you are anti- and find yourself muttering, "More mumbo-jumbo about vibrations and ectoplasm!" just hold your horses and bear with me for a few minutes more.

'Personally, at the moment, I stand uncommitted. I only know what I have read. The author, Dr. Raudive, is not an electronics man, but he has apparently recorded some 72,000 of these voices and a selection of these has been put on to a gramophone record which is on general sale. What is even more important from our standpoint is that he has called in a host of independent opinions, including those from highly qualified physicists and electronics engineers, all of whom verify the claim that voices do appear on the tape, although not all are convinced that they originate from the dead. No one can offer any theory which reconciles known natural laws with the phenomena. The electronics engineers have experienced this mysterious voice production using their own equipment and have weighted in with various circuits of their own devising (this book gives diagrams) which offer improvements on the original Raudive apparatus. Incidentally, it is suggested that videotape might provide a medium for further development work.

'...As for the end products, these are described as "voices which identify themselves, call our names, tell us things that make sense (or sometimes puzzle us); these voices do not originate acoustically and the names they give belong to people we know to have left this earth. The voices are on a tape which can be listened to and heard by everybody. The physicists cannot explain the phenomenon and the psychologists cannot offer an explanation either. Scientific tests have shown (in a Faraday cage, for example) that these voices originate outside the experimenter and are not subject to auto-suggestion or telepathy. Philologists have examined the phenomenon and testified that, although

6

audible and understandable, *the voices are not formed by acoustic means; they are twice the speed of human speech and of a peculiar rhythm which is identical in the 72,000 examples so far examined.*" (My italics.)

'It seems also that the sentences are telegraphese in character and, when the experimenter is multilingual the language may be polyglot—one word perhaps in Swedish, the next in German, the next in English, and so on. Like the messages purporting to emanate from conventional psychic sources, the accent seems to be on identification of friends and relatives who have passed over.

'The sincerity of the book seems beyond question and the near one hundred pages of appendices give much technical detail of the apparatus used, as well as hypotheses regarding the cause of the phenomenon.

'...The theories involving relativity and anti-matter are among those present.

'...One thing is sure, and that is that the problem of the origin of these "voices" cries out for investigation. I know, as well as you, that the whole thing sounds impossible. How can words be derived from a silent microphone? But don't forget that in 1901 it was theoretically impossible for radio waves to cross the Atlantic because no one knew of the existence of the ionosphere. By the same token there are no doubt a lot of things about electronics of which so far we know nothing.'

Ernest Truman came to the end of his reading. Slowly he closed the magazine, removed his spectacles, and wiped his brow with a large white handkerchief. That done, and the spectacles again on his nose, he looked round to see what effect his reading had had.

For moments there were stunned faces around him. Ivan Austin stood with his mouth open. Alice May Cling was clinging to the arm of her girl-friend. Rusty Nales released a deep breath and the profound expression 'Chee! Whaddya-know?' Eva Brick, the girl who packed up the glass tubes, smiled knowingly as she turned to her friend Ivy Covrd, and said, 'Well, well! So Lobsang Rampa has been proved right again. Am I ever glad!'

R. U. Crisp had the last word, though. 'Back to work, folks, you have had your fun. Back to work. This is COST-

ING!' So in ones and twos the staff went back to work as slowly as they could while discussing the matter as fast as they could.

Rest was ended, too, on the edge of the Valley of Lhasa where the trail swept down to the lowlands, and where Lama and acolyte were getting to their feet preparatory to continuing their journey on the reluctant ponies.

Once again the ponies shied away from the boy and, indeed, made fun of him, keeping just, and only just, beyond reach, evading even his most energetic darts in an attempt to grab them. At last the Lama again stepped forward and the ponies came towards him as docile as could be. Once again the Lama and acolyte mounted, and clutching their bundles rode off down the trail.

The Lama rode ahead. Perhaps fifty yards behind him came the acolyte, being favoured by fortune in that his pony wanted to follow his friend, because the acolyte had little control over his steed. But the journey continued between towering rocks, beneath the lips of immense precipices. Gradually they approached the Happy River. Here it was called the River Yaluzangbujiang, but upon leaving Tibet and making a sharp hairpin bend through the mountains it would become the mighty Brahmaputra which, growing in volume and strength, would sweep down to the Bay of Bengal and become one of the most important rivers in India. Now it was a happy river, having some three sources in Tibet, all coming together in Lhasa, in the Valley of Lhasa, and being fed by many, many tributaries in the Valley of Lhasa. Innumerable springs welled up at the foot of Iron Mountain and at the foot of the Potala and formed the Serpent Temple Lake and the Willow Pond and the marshes, and then slowly drained out into the Happy River. Now on the downward slopes beyond the Valley of Lhasa the river was becoming broader, stronger.

The Lama and the acolyte continued their journey, three days, perhaps four days, one loses count of days in a land where time matters not, where there are no clocks, no watches, nothing but the passing of the sun and the phases of the moon to mark the days and the months.

They passed down from the higher mountainous plateaus to the lowlands where the rhododendron trees grew to immense size and the blooms were a mass of flaming colour, each bloom the size of a good cabbage, and the trees of the rhododendron plant itself reaching perhaps twenty-five to thirty feet in height. Here, too, there were many many different plants and trees. The air was steaming, foggy, hot because here the air was trapped in a rocky defile, in a deep rift. On one side was the rockface, and on the other, on the right-hand side, was the rushing river, roaring and screaming as it screeched over gorges and fell a hundred feet at a time over rock lips to go plopping into deep pools below.

Time and again the Lama and the acolyte had to cross and recross and cross again the river on precariously placed bridges made of poles suspended on lian or long strips of creeper plant, strips of creeper as pliant as rope and with the strength of the parent wood. Each time the two ponies had to be blindfolded and led carefully across the bridge, for no pony or horse would cross such a dangerous structure as these temporary bridges.

The young acolyte waddled across one bridge, rubbing his rearmost portion ruefully. 'Oh, Honourable Lama,' he exclaimed, 'having now ridden these days I quite understand why the traders who go to India and return have such a peculiar walk.'

At last, three or four days later, with their barley exhausted and suffering the pangs of hunger, they came in sight of a little lamasery nestling down deep in a valley. At the back a waterfall came tumbling over a cliff edge and passed to the side of the little lamasery, rushing down on the endless journey to the Bay of Bengal.

In front of the lamasery some fifty or sixty monks were gathered looking upwards, shading their eyes against the sun. At last, as the tall Lama rode into their range of vision, they broke into smiles of welcome and the Abbot of the lamasery moved forward with cries of pleasure. Monks seized the ponies and helped Lama and acolyte dismount.

The young acolyte was preening himself here, for was he not one of the acolytes from the Potala in Holy Lhasa? Was he not of the élite of the élite? Was he not accompanying the Great Venerable Lama to give instructions to this lamasery? Then OF COURSE he was worthy of the greatest respect, he was worthy of the respect due to a junior lama at least. So he preened himself and strutted around, then suddenly he remembered he was hungry.

The Abbot was talking animatedly to the Lama, the Lama from the highest centre of lamastic learning. Then all of a sudden the party moved on an impulse into the lamasery where there was hot tea and tsampa. The young acolyte took a hearty swig of tea, and thought the world had come to an end. He coughed and spluttered, and blew tea all over the place. 'Oh, Holy Lama!' he exclaimed in terror. 'Help me, quick!'

The Lama moved to him swiftly and said, 'Do not fear, nothing has happened to you. Remember, we are much lower here and so hot tea is hotter. As I have been trying to tell you, the boiling point of water in Lhasa is quite cool compared to what it is here. Here you will have to wait a little and not drink so quickly. Now, drink again for the temperature will be less by now.' So saying, and smiling, he went back to his discussion with the Abbot and some of the local lamas. The acolyte, feeling rather foolish, very gingerly picked up his drinking bowl and this time cautiously sipped the tea. Yes, it certainly was hot, hotter than anything he had ever tasted before, but it was very pleasant so. And then he turned his attention to the tsampa which also was hot, the first hot tsampa he had tasted in his life.

But already the trumpets were blaring, already there was the sound of the conches. Clouds of incense came wafting out of the temple door, and from nearby came the deep sound of lamastic voices as monks and lamas started their evening service to which the High Lama and the acolyte were now about to go.

That night there was much talk, talk of the doings in Lhasa, talk brought from India by the traders and relayed to the monks, who told the lamas, and then there was the counterpoint of conversation with the lamas and acolytes at this small lamasery. There were tales of the tea planters at Assam, tales of traders from Bhutan, and of course the inevitable stories about the Chinese, about their villainy, about their treachery, about how in the years to come they would invade all this land. The talk went on endlessly. The sun set early here, and the deep gloom pervaded this dark cleft of the valley.

Here in the night there was much more noise. There were many more birds, many more animals than in the vicinity of Lhasa. This was the lowland and the young acolyte found great difficulty in breathing, he found the air too moist, too thick. He found that he was drowning in air, and restlessly he prowled about, finding it quite impossible to sleep in the confines of a communal monks' dormitory.

Out in the open there was the pleasant scent of flowers wafted on the cool night breeze. Animals called and night birds went flapping off, darker shadows against a dark sky. At his left the Happy River plunged over a rock edge and went rushing down in a splather of white froth and foam, dislodging rocks and pebbles in its hurry to get down to the sea. The young boy sat on a rock by the side of the waterfall and thought of all the things that had happened to him, he thought of his life at Chakpori, he thought of his life in the Potala, and now, on the morrow, he thought, he was going to have to attend lectures by his beloved Lama on breathing.

Suddenly the night became darker still, the wind turned chill and, being moist, seemed to strike through to the bones. Shivering, the young boy rose to his feet and hastened into the lamasery to sleep.

The light of the new day was much slower in reaching this little lamasery hidden in the sheltered valley, encompassed on every side by towering rocks heavily clothed with sub-tropical vegetation—for in this valley with its closed-in atmosphere the temperatures rose rapidly—the rays of light from the sun were cut off until almost mid-morning, and here there was a gloominess, a steamy gloominess.

High overhead the sky was of pellucid luminescence, the light of the newborn day. No longer did the stars shine brightly, no longer were there rays of the setting moon. All was bright, and yet in this valley the young acolyte found it oppressive, stifling, he felt drowning in air, as it were. He rose and made his way from the dormitory out into the open, out into what to him was the grey light of day. Greyness filtering down through mist or fog. Greyness accentuated by the leaping spray which, because of the dullness, showed no scintillating rainbows.

The young acolyte felt he was alone in a sleeping world. He thought how lazy they were down in this quiet backwater of religion. So he wandered to sit by the side of the waterfall. There he reflected upon some of the things he had learned at the Potala and at Chakpori, he thought of some of the things he had learned about breathing. He thought, too, that this day there would be more to be learned about breathing and now he decided he would do some breathing exercises.

He sat bolt upright with his spine erect, and he breathed deeply and he exhaled deeply. He breathed deeply and exhaled deeply. He worked hard at it, really hard at it. Of a sudden he found he was out of his body, he found a most peculiar sensation. The next thing he knew was that he was lying on the ground with the High Lama bending over him.

'Boy,' said the voice of the Lama, 'have you forgotten all that I have told you? Here, remember, the air is thicker than that to which you are accustomed. Do you not know that you were working at this and you have made yourself drunk with too much oxygen?'

He sprinkled cold water on the young acolyte's face and shaven head, causing him to shudder with horror. Now he would have to dry himself! 'I warned you,' said the Lama, 'that one should not overdo deep breathing at the start. Even if it does appear to be beneficial, do not overdo it. Certainly you have been doing it in thicker air and really working at it—I saw you from the window! Your lungs were going in and out like bellows—well, I came just in time or you would have toppled into the gorge and then I should have had no one with me to make the ponies amused. But come, rise to your feet, we will return to the lamasery.' The Lama reached down and helped the boy arise. Together they walked into the lamasery. The boy felt immensely better at the sight of tea and tsampa already prepared. He was even more cheered at the sight of some other things, some sort of fruits which were strange to him.

'Oh!' he said to another boy near him. 'We do not have anything like those in Lhasa. We have nothing but tea and tsampa, nothing more at all.'

The boy smiled at him and replied, 'Oh, we don't do so badly here.' Smugly—'the peasants bring here for our services, you know. We go and toss out a blessing or two and we get some fruits or some vegetables. It eases the eternal tsampa. Personally I would rather be here than at Lhasa, conditions are much more relaxed.'

They sat down cross-legged on the floor in front of the small tables, and then taking their bowls they put in tea and tsampa. For sime time all was silent except for the voice of the Reader who, from a high position looking out across the dining hall, read from the Sacred Works during mealtimes because it was not considered fit that monks should pay too much attention to their food.

'Be careful how you eat those fruits,' muttered the boy to whom the young acolyte had spoken before. 'If you eat too many of those you'll wonder what happened to you inside. It's not the going down which causes the trouble, it's the after-effects.'

'Oh!' exclaimed the young acolyte in very considerable dismay. 'Oh indeed! I have had five of them already. Come to think of it I do feel a bit peculiar inside.'

The boy who gave him the warning laughed and reached for another of the fruits himself.

At last all had finished eating and the Reader had finished his Lesson. The Abbot rose to his feet and said that on this occasion the Great Honourable Lama from Lhasa, from the Holy of Holies, the Potala, had come especially to lecture on breathing and on health, and after any who had any problems with health were invited to discuss the matter with the Lama from Lhasa. They all filed out of the place of the dining and moved instead into the Temple proper where there was more room.

The Lama bade them all be seated in comfort. The small boys were in the front, the young monks were next and in the rear were the lamas, all sitting in orderly rows.

For some time the Lama gave basic instructions and then he said, 'I must emphasise again that it is not at all necessary for you to sit in the Lotus Position or to sit in any position which is uncomfortable. You must at all times sit in a position which is comfortable, a position wherein your spine is erect, because only then can you derive the maximum benefit. Remember, also, that by day you sit with your palms upwards so that you may absorb the good influences of the sun throughout the day, but when you do these exercises after sunset you will have your palms facing downwards because then you come under the influence of the moon.

88

'But now let us repeat that you have to find your pulse. You place your fingers on your left wrist so that you determine your pulse count, so that you may know for how long you can breathe in or breathe out. The average will be one, two, three, four (in), one, two, three, four (out). Say this to yourself out loud six or seven times, and then get the actual beat fixed firmly in your mind so that when you are not feeling your pulse you are still quite able to sense what your pulse beat is. This will take a few days of practice, and after you have practised it for a few days you will find that you can tell your pulse count by a vibration within your body, you will not have to feel your pulse any more.

'First of all you must inhale, always, of course, with the mouth closed. You inhale deeply to the count of four. It is vital that you breathe in absolutely smoothly without any jerks whatever. Beginners tend to draw in breaths to the count of four and that is harmful; they must breathe in smoothly at the count, the mental count, of four. Then when you have counted four you should have a complete lungful of breath, so then you breathe out to a count of four pulses. Do this for a time, and after several days you will be able to take in air for more than four pulses, you may be able to do six or eight. But you should never force yourself, always do it so that it is well within your capabilities.'

The Lama looked around and studied the small boys, the monks, and the Lamas, all sitting there, all with their palms facing upwards, all breathing in their own particular rhythm. The Lama nodded his satisfaction and raised his hand for them to cease the exercise.

'Now,' he said, 'we will do the next stage of this because we do precisely as you have been doing but now after inhaling you will retain your breath. First of all, then, let us inhale for four heartbeats. Then you will retain that breath for two heartbeats, and you will then exhale over another four heartbeats. The purpose of this particular matter, of this particular breathing pattern, is to purify the blood. It also helps increase the good condition of the stomach and the liver. It strengthens the nervous system when carried out properly. Remember, too, that our basic is four, two, four. That is merely an average, you must not be a slave to these. Your average could easily be six, three, six, or five, three, five. It is exactly that which is most suitable and most strain-free for you.'

He stood watching while the assembly breathed in, retained their breath, and breathed out. He watched them do it ten, twenty, twenty-five times. Then, again nodding his satisfaction, he held up his hand.

'Now we will go a step farther. I have seen particularly among the younger men examples of poor posture. You men and boys just slouching around. Now, that makes for bad health. When you are walking you should walk to your heartbeat and to your breath. Let us practice it this way; first you must stand erect, not bending over forwards, not tottering over backwards—erect, with your feet together and with your spine straight. First exhale as much as you can, squeeze every bit of air out of your lungs. Then start to walk and at the same instant take a really deep breath. It doesn't matter if you use the left foot or the right foot, but make sure it is a really deep breath. At the same time take a slow rhythmic step. You will walk in time to your heartbeat. You are going to inhale over four heartbeats. During that time you will take four steps. But then you have to take four more steps over the four heartbeats which it takes to exhale. Do this for six consecutive sets of four, but remember with particular care that your breathing must be absolutely smooth, it must not be done in pattern with your steps; that is, you do not pump breath in in four steps as you walk, you should inhale as smoothly as you can.'

The High Lama from Lhasa suppressed a secret smile of amusement as he watched boys, monks, and lamas strutting around trying to carry out the breathing execises. But satisfied that they were doing it correctly he said, 'Now let us remember that there are many systems of breathing and we have to breathe in a manner which will enable us to fulfil a certain task because breathing is more than stuffing our lungs with air. Correct breathing can refresh us and can actually tone up our organs. The breathing system I have been showing you is known as the complete breathing system. It is a breathing system which purifies the blood, it helps the stomach and other organs. It also helps to overcome colds.' He stopped and looked around at certain sniffers, and resumed, 'Here in this, the lowland of Tibet, colds are rife, and nothing much seems to have been done about it. By using that correct breathing system which I have been teaching you, you can overcome colds. Now here is another system in which you will retain your breath for longer than normal. Sit down, please, with your spine erect, but the rest of you relaxed.'

He stood waiting while the men settled themselves again, arranged their robes around them, and sat with their palms facing upwards. Then he resumed:

'First of all you will do your complete breath, that is, that which we have been doing so far. Then you will retain the air as long as you can without any strain. After that you will exhale through the open mouth rather vigorously as if the air is distasteful, as if you are trying to shoot it away from you as violently as you can. So, let us have it again; first you inhale for four heartbeats. Then you retain the air which you have just inhaled for as long as you can without suffering discomfort. Next you expel the air as vigorously as you can through the open mouth. You will find if you do this a few times that your health will definitely improve.'

The Lama stood watching his pupils making sure that they were doing it correctly. Then spotting one elderly man turning a bluish colour he hastened to him and said, 'Now, my brother, you have been trying too hard. All these exercises must be done in a natural manner, in an easy manner. There must be no strain, there must be no effort in it. To breathe is natural, and if there is effort or strain then you are not getting good effects from that breathing. You, my brother, are using the wrong rhythm. You are trying to force yourself to take in more air than elderly lungs can take in. Be careful, do all this easily, without strain, and you will feel better.'

So for the morning the boys, the monks, and the Lamas did their breathing exercises. At last, to the delight of the young acolyte, the lessons were ended and he and the others were free to go out again into the open where the noontime sun was now striking down into the valley, lighting up the gloom and, unfortunately, increasing the heat. Insects buzzed vigorously around, and the poor young acolyte jumped and jumped again as insects to which he was not accustomed attacked him in the most vulnerable portions of his anatomy.

CHAPTER SEVEN

Lady St. John de Tawfe-Nause, of Hellzapoppin Hall, sat in solitary grandeur at the head of the immense table in her breakfast-room. Fastidiously she toyed with the thin slice of rye-bread toast before her. Delicately she raised a tea-cup to her well-shaped lips, then on an impulse put it down in the saucer and hurried off to her ornate writing-desk. Selecting a sheet of writing paper bearing the crest of a famous Norman (really he was named Guillaume!) ancestor, and consisting of a bald-headed cuckoo rampant (given because he was a bit 'cuckoo' and always went at a thing bald-headed), she started to write with a pen which had been pinched from one of the Duke of Wellington's footmen who had pinched it from a tavern off Fleet Street.

'So you are the author of "The Third Eye",' she wrote. 'I wish to see you. Meet me at my Club and be sure to wear civilised Western dress. I have my position to consider . . .'

Bertie E. Cutzem, one of the leading surgeons of England, member of most of the Learned Societies, Fellow of THIS and THAT, *bon vivant*, clubman, and advocate of Privileges for the Privileged Classes, sat in his office, chin in hand. At last, after profound cogitation, he seized a sheet of discreetly-monogrammed paper and started:

'I have just read "The Third Eye",' he wrote, 'and I know that all you write is true. My son has marked occult powers and he knows from other sources that you write the truth. I should like to meet you, but PLEASE return this letter as my colleagues would laugh at me . . .'

The wealthy Californian film-maker sat in his palatial office surrounded by his almost naked harem. Sylva Skreen was now a household word. Years before he had come to the States from Greece, and like hot grease he ran away from the hot time if he stayed in Greece. The police

92

wanted to put him in the 'cooler'. So, off to America he dashed and landed in 'Frisco with a hole in his pants and holes in his soles. His soul was not in too good a condition either.

Now the Great Man, Sylva Skreen, sat in his office and tried to write a letter without his secretary typing it. Idly he sat and twirled his solid gold pen—the one studded with diamonds and with the whacking great ruby at the end opposite the nib. His face contorted, he fumbled with his fractured, nay, SHATTERED English. At last, when the suspense was becoming painful, he reached out and seized a gaudy sheet of paper and started to write.

In effect, the letter demanded the presence of the Author of 'The Third Eye' so that the Great Greek God of the Silver Screen could have his fortune told and perhaps increased. He enclosed the money for return air fare. With extreme pain he wrote a cheque and enclosed it in the envelope. A minion rushed to mail the missive.

Sylva Skreen sat mulling in his office. Pain assailed him in his pocket-book. 'What have I done?' he cried. 'My money she is spent. I go foolish. No matter, I now go wise.' He heaved his swelly belly up so that it was supported by the expensive desk, quickly he called his secretary. 'To the Author of "The Third Eye",' he dictated. 'You have my money. You I don't want. My money I do want. And if you don't return my money fast I tell the Press you took my money, so you send my money fast, eh?'

A functionary functioned at top speed to hasten the despatch of the Missive to the Author. At last, in the fullness of time—for the mails are very slow—Sylva Skreen, the Greek, could rub his greasy hands on his returned money.

In far away Uruguay the Author of many books received a letter from Seattle, U.S.A. 'I am told you want to return to North America,' stated this letter from a very wealthy man. 'But you do not have the money for your fare. Now, I will make a very good proposition to you. I will pay your fare to Seattle and I will keep you for the rest of your life. You will have one room and your food. You should not want many clothes. In return you must turn over everything you have to me and you must legally sign over all book rights to me. Then I will market your books and keep your royalties in reurn for keeping you.' The Author uttered an unmentionable word in an unmentionable manner about that unmentionable person.

The door resounded to a thunderous knocking. A knocking repeated as it was not instantly opened. Hurrying footsteps, the sound of the door opening. 'Choust a peek I take, no?' said a thick guttural voice. 'Von Lama I gom to see. In you shute led me gom, yes?' The sound of voices and the volume of one increasing: 'Mine freund, she say you go she say. You say you vant for the Lama to see she say. Upon your doorstep I vill live mitt mineself and vill stay yet already. You tell him Vilhemina Cherman she is here, no?'

Midnight in Montreal. Across the water the lights of the skyscrapers of Drapeau's Dream were reflecting in the unruffled waters of the Port. Motionless at anchor the ships rested placidly the advent of another day. To the left, where Windmill Basin afforded moorings for the tugs the water was suddenly roiled as a small boat got under way to meet a late-coming freighter. Atop the tallest building a rotating beacon sent probing fingers into the night sky. A jet plane whistled across the city as it escaped from the confines of the International Airport.

Midnight in Montreal. The household was wrapped in sleep. Sleep which suddenly was shattered by the insistent ringing of the door bell. Clothes were quickly donned and the door was opened. Only dire emergency would prompt such a long ring at such an hour, surely? 'Rampa?' asked a gruff French-Canadian voice. 'Dr. Rampa live here?' Two big men pushed their way in and stood looking around. 'Police. Fraud Squad,' said one at length.

'Who is this Dr. Rampa? What does he do? Where is he?' asked the other. Questions—questions—questions. But then a counter-question. 'What do you want? Why have you come here?' The two policemen looked at each other blankly. The senior of the two, without even asking permission, strode to the telephone and dialled a number. There followed a rapid-fire exchange of the French-Canadian version of the French language. At last the phone was put down and the senior policeman said, 'Uh, we were told to come here, called in our police car. We were not told why. Now the Superintendent says a man called him from Alabama and said to tell Dr. Rampa to call him FAST. It is

94

urgent. Do it NOW!'

Uneasily the two policemen stood and looked at each other. They shifted their weight from one leg to the other. At last, the senior said, 'We go, you telephone immediately, yes?' They turned and stumped out of the room. Soon there came the sound of their car starting and zooming along the road far in excess of the legal speed limit. Then came the ringing of the telephone. 'Superintendent of Police here. HAVE YOU TELEPHONED YET??? The man said it was urgent, a matter of life and death.' There was a click and the call was ended.

The letter plopped in together with about seventy others. The envelope was of a violent mauve hue with improbable flowers fore and aft. The paper, when unfolded, was of the same horrendous colour, worsened by hanging wreaths of flowers entwined all around the edge. 'God is Love!' proclaimed a banner across the top. The Author wrinkled his nose at the stink coming from it. The 'scent' used must have come from a diseased skunk who had died after eating, he thought.

The letter said: 'I am Auntie Macassar, and I Tell Fortunes and Do Much Good. (Five bucks a question or a bigger Love Offering.) Now I have read your books and I want you to be my Guide. It will do me a POWER of good in my advertising. Send me your letter agreeing, fast, because I want to advertise it.'

'Rampa has gone commercial!' shrieked the letter. 'I know you are a fake because you run businesses and make money.' The poor wretched Author lay back in his bed and tried to work THAT one out; did it mean that all people engaged in business were fakes? Or what? 'Oh well,' he thought, 'I will make it clear in my next book.'

Ladies and gentlemen, children, cats of all description. Listen to this statement, proclamation, and declaration. I, Tuesday Lobsang Rampa using my own and legal name and my only name, depose thus:— I have NO business interests. I am not engaged in business of any kind except that of Author. I do NOT endorse any incense, mail-order firm, or what-nots. Certain people are using names such as 'The Third Eye', but I wrote a BOOK by that name, not started a mail order company. A mail order company which I do NOT endorse.

Ladies and gentlemen, children, cats of all description. I have no disciples, students, representatives, followers, pupils, business interests, or any agents other than my LITERARY agents. Nor have I written any books 'refused by publishers because of their forbidden knowledge'. Someone may be trying to part you from your hard-earned money; (I wish I COULD do it!) so you have been warned ... by me.

The Author lay back and dwelt upon the difficulties of being an author. 'You must not use the word "crummy",' wrote one. 'It is Bad Language.' 'You must not use "I",' wrote another. 'It makes your readers identify themselves too closely with you. That's BAD!' 'You must not say you are the "Old Man",' complains yet another. 'I don't like to read it.' And so the letters go on. So the Author (who else?) lay back and pondered upon the past and worried unduly perhaps about the future. Failing health, failing this and failing that ...

The door was pushed open and a beautiful furry form jumped lightly on the bed where the Author was lying thinking of the past. 'Hey, Guv!' she said in her best Siamese Cat Telepathic Voice. 'And how about the book you are supposed to be writing? My! You will never get it finished if you think of those silly ninnies, the Fairweather Friends. Forget 'em!' she commanded sternly.

Fat Taddy strolled in and sat in a vagrant patch of sunlight. 'Food?' she enquired. 'Did someone mention FOOD?' The Author smiled at them and said, 'Well, cats, we have to finish this book and we have to answer some of those questions which come pouring in. Questions, questions, QUESTIONS! So let us start.' He reached out for the typewriter with the sticking 'i' and dragged it towards him. Now, where is that first question?

The difficulty is that just as people beget people so do answers beget questions. The more question is answered the more questions seem to arise. Now here is a question which seems to have troubled a lot of people. The question is— What IS this Overself? Why does the Overself make me suffer so much? How CAN it be just that I have to suffer so when I do not know why I have to suffer? It doesn't make sense, it destroys my faith in religion. It destroys my faith in a God. Can you explain this to me?

The Author lay back and contemplated a passing ship.

Once again a ship was coming bringing all manner of goods from Japan, but that was not getting on with the book, was it? The Author reluctantly turned back and started to work again.

Yes, of course such a question can be answered, but first of all we have to agree to certain terms of reference because think of trying to discuss with a fish in the depths of the ocean the thoughts and reactions of space men in orbit around the moon. How could we get it over to a fish which always lived on the bottom of the ocean what life was like on the surface of the ocean? How would we explain life in London, Montreal, Tokyo, or even New York where there are many queer fish already? But, beyond this, how would we explain to our seabed-dwelling fish what happens to a space ship going around the moon? It would be just about impossible, wouldn't it? So let us make an assumption, let us imagine something different.

Let us imagine that the Overself is not the Overself any more, it is just a brain. So, we get a lot of brains floating about somewhere, and then the brain decides it wants to know something, it wants to experience something other than pure thought. By 'pure' thought it is meant that the thought is an insubstantial thing and does not concern itself with pure or impure in the moral sense of the meaning.

This particular brain, then, has the stirrings of ambition. It wants to know things, it wants to know what things are like on Earth, is the thirteenth candle hotter than the twelfth candle? And what is 'hot', anyway, and then, what is a candle? The brain decides to find out, so the brain finds a body. Forget for the moment that the brain has to be born first, but this brain gets itself fixed inside a skull, a thick bony box in which it floats in a special liquid which prevents it from experiencing mechanical shocks, which keeps it moist, and which helps to feed it. Here we have this brain in its bony box. Now, a brain is quite without feeling, that is, if a surgeon wants to operate on a brain he just gives a local anaesthetic to the skin and flesh outside the skull, and then he makes an incision nearly all the way around the head. Then a saw is used to saw through the top of the skull which can then be peeled back like taking the top off a hard-boiled egg. It is important to remember that one experiences pain only in the skin, the flesh, and the bone. The brain is not sensitive to pain. So when the surgeon has got the lid off, so to speak, he can poke and probe and cut into the brain without any anaesthetic being used.

Our brain is like the Overself. It has no sensation of its own. So let us go back to the brain in the skull which is wanting experience. We must keep in mind, though, that we are using the simile of the brain to stand in place of the Overself which, being a many-dimensional object, is harder to comprehend.

The brain wants to know about sensations. The brain is blind, it is deaf, it cannot detect a scent, it has no feeling. So we make a lot of puppets. One pair of puppets are extended in the form of eyes, the eyes come open and the brain receives impressions from the eyes. As we all know, a newborn baby cannot understand what the impressions mean. A newborn baby fumbles and obviously does not comprehend what he is seeing, but with experience the impressions received from the eyes mean something to the brain.

But that could be improved upon. We want more than a picture. We can see a thing, but what does it feel like? Does it have a scent, does it have a sound? Other puppets are put out and they call themselves ears. They catch vibrations of a lower frequency than the eyes can receive. They are still vibrations just as sight is receiving vibrations. But the ears pick up vibrations and with practice the brain can understand that these vibrations mean something, they may mean pleasant music, they may mean unpleasant music, they may mean speech, a form of communication.

Well, having seen and heard a thing, does it smell? The best way is to move puppets to form an olfactory organ. Then the poor wretched Overself, which here we are calling the brain, may sometimes wish that there was no sense of smell, it depends on what kind of scent the woman is wearing!

To go farther—what does a thing feel like? We do not know the meaning of terms such as 'hard' and 'soft' unless we have feeling, so the Overself, or, in this case, the brain puts out more puppets; arms, hands, fingers. We have a finger and a thumb so that we can pick up a small article. We have fingers which we may move over an object to know whether it is easily compressed or not compressible, to know whether it is soft or if it is hard. We know if it is blunt or if it is sharp through our fingers.

Sometimes a thing will hurt. We touch an article and it gives us a most unpleasant sensation. It might be hot, it might be cold, it might be sharp or rough. Those sensations create pain and the pain warns us to be careful of such things in the future. But why should the fingers revile themselves or revile a God because they are merely carrying out their allotted purpose, the purpose of feeling?

A bricklayer may get hard fingers through handling bricks. A surgeon may get very sensitive fingers because of the necessary delicacy of touch required in his job. To do bricklaying would harm the surgeon's fingers, but surgery would be difficult for the bricklayer because his fingers would be coarsened by bricklaying.

Every organ has to experiment, has to endure. Ears may be shocked by a very loud noise, a nose may be offended by a particularly unpleasant odour, but these organs are designed to withstand such shocks. You burn a finger—well, the finger heals and we know better next time.

Our brains file away all information. It is locked in the nine-tenths of the sub-conscious. Our involuntary nervous system will react on information supplied by the sub-conscious to prevent us from coming to any great harm. For instance, if you try to walk on the top of a high building you will experience fear which is the way the sub-conscious communicates to the involuntary nervous system that it should pour secretion into the blood and make one jump back.

This is in the ordinary physical sense, but just think in a much higher dimension how the Overself is unable to receive any knowledge of the Earth without putting puppets on the Earth. These puppets are humans, humans who can get burns, cuts, stunned, all manner of things can happen to the human, and all the sensations and impressions are returned to the Overself by way of the Silver Cord in much the same way as impressions received by finger and thumb of the human body are relayed by way of the nerves to the brain, the sensory nerves.

We, then, are justified in calling ourselves extensions of an Overself which is so very highly rarefied, so very highly insulated, so very highly evolved that it has to depend on us to pick up impressions of what happens on this Earth. If we do something wrong, then we get a metaphorical kick in the pants. It is not a devilish God which is afflicting us, persecuting us and tempting us. It is our own crass stupidity. Or maybe some people touch a thing and find it hurts, so they touch it again to find out why it hurts, and then they touch it again to find out how the hurt may be cured or overcome. And then they may touch it yet again to see if the matter has been finally overcome.

You may get a very good person who gets a lot of pain and you—the onlooker—may think it is unfair that such a person should have such suffering, or you may think that the person concerned is paying back an exceedingly hard Kharma, he must have been a fiend in a previous life, you may consider. But you would be wrong. How do you not know that the person is not enduring the pain and suffering in order to see how pain and suffering can be eliminated for those who come after? Do not think that it is always paying back Kharma. It may possibly be accumulating good Kharma.

There is a God, a good God, a fair God. But of course God is not the same as a human and it is useless to attempt to comprehend what IS God when most people cannot even comprehend their own Overself. Just as you cannot comprehend your Overself, nor can you comprehend the God of your Overself.

Here is a question which already has been answered in previous books, but still comes up regularly, with monotonous regularity, in fact:

People want to know about their Guide, their Master, their Keeper, their Guardian Angel, etc. A person writes and says, 'Oh, I have an old Red Indian as my Guide. I wish I could see him. I know he is a Red Indian because he is so wise. How can I see him?'

Now, let us get this straight once and for all; people do not have Red Indians, Black Indians, White Indians, or Tibetans dead or alive as Guides. Actually there would not be enough Tibetans, for instance, to go round. It's like everyone saying, 'Oh, I was Cleopatra in my last life!' There is no word of truth in it. Actually the alleged Guide is just the Overself who really is our Guide. It is like sitting in a car; YOU are the car's Overself. You stamp on the pedal and, if you are lucky and don't have a new American car, the car will go. You stamp on another pedal and the car stops, and if you pull a certain thing and if you are watching what you are doing you won't run into anything. But no one else but you is driving that car. In the same way you control yourself, you and your Overself.

Many people have the idea that those who have passed from the Earth are just bubbling over with enthusiasm to just sit at somebody's shoulder and guide them throughout the days of their life, prevent them from falling by the roadside, telling them what to do, and all the rest of it. But just think for yourself; you have neighbours, possibly you get on with those neighbours, possibly you don't, but anyway the time has come, you are going to move to the other side of the world. If you are in England you are going to move to Australia. If you are in North America you are going to move to, let us say, Siberia. Well, you move, you are busy with your moving, you are busy settling in to your new address, you are busy with your work at your new location, you are busy making fresh contacts. Do you really stop to telephone Tom, Dick, and Harry, and Mary, Martha, and Matilda, or whatever their names may be? You don't, you know. You have forgotten all about them. And so do people on the Other Side.

People who have left this Earth are not just sitting on clouds playing their harps and plucking feathers out of wings, etc., etc. They have a job to do; they leave this Earth, they have a period of recuperation and then they get busy on something else. Quite frankly they do not have time to be Spirit Guides and all that rubbish.

Many, many times entities who are not human will be able to intercept the thoughts of a human and, under certain conditions, will give the impression of being a Spirit Guide.

Let us consider the case of these seances; here we have a group of people who are hoping for communication with those who have passed over. They are a group of people who are all thinking along the same lines. It is not just one person idly thinking, these people are going to some special place for a special purpose, and they are all sub-consciously willing that a message shall be given. So in the astral world there are drifting forms who may be thought forms, or they may be just entities who have not been humans and never will be humans. They are just masses of energy responding to certain stimuli.

These entities, whatever their origin—but certainly they are not human—drift around and soon gravitate to any source which attracts them. If people are thinking strongly about a message from the dead, then these entities will quite automatically be attracted to such a group, and there they will hover around and stretch out pseudopods which, of course, are hands and fingers made of energy, and they will touch a brain or part of a brain, or touch a cheek, and the person receiving such a touch will be sure that he or she is being touched by a spirit because the pseudopods they put out are similar to the pseudopods put out of ectoplasm.

These entities are often mischievous, and they are very, very alert in the same way that monkeys are alert. The entities float around, sort of bouncing from brain to brain, and when they get to some nice juicy item of information which is being radiated from a brain they can cause a sensitive, that is a genuine Medium, to speak. They give a message which at least one person knows to be true because it is in that person's consciousness, but none of them seem to think of the thought form just picking brains. It must be made very, very clear indeed that not all these manifestations are genuine.

We all know what it is like on Hallowe'en when children go about with masks and costumes, and pretend to be something. That is how these thought forms, these entities, behave. They are really things of limited intelligence and they are, quite genuinely, parasites. They will feed upon anything that believes in them.

Under certain conditions a person can have what they believe to be manifestations. They can be sure that they have the spirit of old Aunt Fanny who fell down three flights of stairs and broke her leg and died after it, hanging around advising them because she is so conscience-stricken because of the way she ignored them when she was on the Earth. Well, actually, this is nothing of the sort. The person at the seance might unconsciously have been sending out pictures of Aunt Fanny and her broken leg, thinking what a bad-tempered old biddy she was, and so the mischievous entity will tune-in on that and will alter things around a bit, making sure that they are entirely plausible, and then Aunt Fanny 'comes through' as a person who is sorry she was so obnoxious to her brilliant niece or nephew and now she wants to stay with them for ever or longer, and protect them from everything.

It is really amazing that humans on Earth rather scorn the Red man, rather sneer at the 'Indian' Indians and sometimes tend to disbelieve the authenticity of Tibetan Lamas, yet as soon as these people die the scoffer immediately reverses and thinks that the ones who have been so abused are going to rush back and sit on their shoulders and guide them through life, protect them from all the troubles of life. Well, they've got another think coming. All they have, as already stated, is some incubi hanging around pretending to be something quite different.

Your friends on the other side of the world, how often do you get in touch with them? How often do you help THEM? How often did you help them when they were your neighbours? Now, think—a person passes over from this life, and you didn't even know of their existence when they were on this Earth, so, quite frankly, why do you think they are suddenly going to take such a vast interest in you? Why do you think that some Tibetan Lama or Red Indian Chief is going to drop everything he is doing on the Other Side and rush to be with you for the rest of your life? Somebody at whom you probably scoffed when he was on Earth, or more probably did not even know that he existed.

We must be logical about it. Many people believe they have a Spirit Guide because they feel insecure, because they feel lonely, because they are sure they cannot manage without help. And so, partly, they invent a father figure or a mother figure who is always with them protecting them from their own folly and from the ill-will of others.

Another reason for this belief in Spirit Guides is that sometimes people hear or think they hear a mysterious voice talking to them. What they actually hear is a form of telephone conversation with their own Overself. This is relayed by way of the Silver Cord. It is amplified by the etheric and sometimes reproduced as vibrations by the aura. Sometimes, too, a person will feel a throbbing on the forehead just between the eyes but slightly above the eyes. That is caused when a conversation is going on between the sub-conscious of the human on Earth and the Overself, and the one-tenth conscious is trying to listen in but not being able to do so, and instead getting a throbbing which is the same as the telephone girl saying that the number is engaged.

We have to manage on our own, every one of us. It is wrong to join cults and groups and gaggles. When we leave this Earth we have to go to the Hall of Memories alone. It is useless for us to go to where we judge ourselves and say to our Overselves, 'Oh, the secretary of the Society for Hotter Hot Dogs told me that I should do this or I should not do that.' We have to stand alone, and if Man is to evolve Man must be alone. If we are going to settle in groups and gangs and cults—well, that is several steps backwards because when we join a group or a cult or a society, then we are limited to progress at the rate of the slowest person there. The individualist, the one who wants to get on, the one who is evolved goes alone—always.

In passing, an interesting letter was received two days ago. It said, 'I have been a Member of the ... for forty-four years, and I must confess that I did not learn so much in all that time as I have learned from one of your books.'

CHAPTER EIGHT

The Old Author lay on his bed by the side of the window looking out across the almost deserted Port of Montreal. Ships were not coming so frequently now. There had been so many strikes, thefts, and other unpleasant happenings that many shipping lines were by-passing the Port of Montreal.

The Old Author lay there watching very sparse river traffic, but watching very busy traffic on the road going over to Man and His World, a place which he had no desire to visit. The sun was shining in and the young Girl Cat, Miss Cleopatra, was resting with arms folded on his legs.

She turned to face him and grinning like the proverbial Cheshire cat she said, 'Guv, why is it that humans will not believe that animals can talk?'

'Well, Clee,' responded the Author, 'humans have to have everything proved, they have to hold things in their hot little hands and pull it to pieces so that they can say, "Well, it might have worked once but it certainly doesn't now." But you and I know that cats talk, so what does it matter what anyone else thinks?'

Miss Cleopatra turned the matter over in her mind for a little, her ears twitched and she delicately washed a paw. 'Guv,' she said, 'why do humans not realise that THEY are the ones who are dumb? All animals talk by telepathy. Why not humans?'

Well, the answer to that is rather difficult and the Author was rather reticent about giving it. But—'Now look, Clee,' he replied, 'humans are different in that they never take a thing on trust. You know there is telepathy and I know there is telepathy, but if other people don't know it for some strange reason, then there is nothing that we can do to convince them. Now is there?'

The Author leaned back and smiled his love upon the

Little Girl Cat, his so constant companion.

Miss Cleopatra looked straight at him and thought back, 'Oh, but there is a way, there is a way, you have just been reading about it!'

The Author's eyebrows went up so high that he almost had some hair on the top of his head after all, which was quite a change after so many years of being bald. But then he thought of a book he had been reading about some experiments.

It seems that there were two researchers called R. Allen and Beatrice Gardner, and they were working at the University of Nevada. These two, a husband and wife team, were considering all the problems in teaching animals to speak and wondering why it was apparently impossible to teach animals to speak. The more they thought about it the more puzzling it seemed to them.

Of course apparently they overlooked the most obvious reason which is that animals do not have the necessary mechanism for speaking English or Spanish or French. Possibly they can grunt like some bad-tempered Germans do, but anyway, we are not dealing with Germans, bad-tempered or good.

The Gardners—they are husband and wife—made a different approach to the problem. They realised that chimpanzees managed to convey meaning to each other, and so they studied chimpanzees for a time. They came to the conclusion that many chimpanzees conversed by means of signs in a manner similar to that employed by those who are born deaf.

These people secured a chimpanzee and the animal was given the freedom of the house, and was treated much the same as a human would be treated, or perhaps possibly a little better because many humans do not treat other humans too well, do they? But that is beside the point. These people treated their chimpanzee as a complete member of the family, it had toys, love, and one important thing extra.

The humans in front of the chimpanzee conversed only by sign language. After many months she was able to convey her meanings (yes, it was a female chimpanzee) without particular difficulty.

They taught this chimpanzee for some two years, and she

learned signs for hats, shoes, and all sorts of other articles of clothing, together with many, many other words. She was also able to convey when she wanted something sweet or when she wanted something to drink. The experiment seems to have been quite a success. It is not over yet, by any means, but animals lack the necessary vocal chord equipment to speak in the manner of humans. Possibly they would have difficulty in parsing and deciding on the correct tenses, but when humans are too stupid to be able to converse by telepathy then no doubt the animal will have to converse by means of signs. It is a fact, a demonstrable fact, that Miss Cleopatra and Miss Tadalinka can make their wants and wishes known even to people who are not telepathic. With the Author, of course, there was complete *rapport*, and Author and Siamese cats are able to converse with possibly greater facility than between two non-telepathic humans.

Miss Tadalinka sauntered in and said, 'You two talking about food?'

'No, Tads,' replied Miss Cleopatra, 'we are talking about conversing with humans, and we think we are very fortunate in having the Guv tell our wants and save us the trouble of having to use sign language.'

Miss Cleo looked up at the Author and said, 'You should be out, you know, you haven't been out for weeks. Why don't you get in your chair and go down into the grounds? It's a quiet day, there aren't many people about.'

The Author looked out of the window. The sun was shining, there wasn't much wind, but then he looked at the typewriter and the blank sheets of paper. He muttered an appropriate imprecation about the paper and the typewriter and struggled off the bed and into the electrically-propelled wheelchair.

It is rather difficult getting along a corridor, getting out of a door and into an elevator when one needs hands to use an electric wheelchair, but it can be done. The Author went down from the ninth floor to ground level. On ground level he decided to travel through the grounds and sit for a while by the side of the river.

Along the concrete street he went, and down the ramp at the end leading to the car-park. Crossing the car-park, he went up another little ramp to the sidewalk, a sidewalk which was quite, quite deserted. Gently he pushed the lever forward and the chair moved ahead at walking speed.

Suddenly there was a roar of a racing car engine and a swoosh as a big car came on the wrong side of the road and a harsh voice said, 'Stop!'

The Author looked around in some surprise, and as he did so a police sergeant and a police detective jumped out of a police car while the police driver was half hanging out of the driver's window.

'Oh, good gracious!' thought the Author. 'Whatever is wrong now?'

The police sergeant and the detective hurried forward and stood in front of the now stationary wheelchair. The sergeant glowered down with his hands on his hips and demanded, 'You that author fellow?'

'Yes,' was the reply.

The sergeant looked at the detective and the detective said abruptly, 'You should not be out alone. You look as if you're going to die at any minute.'

The Author was understandably somewhat surprised at such a remark, such a greeting, and he replied mildly, 'Die? We're all going to die some time. I'm getting along all right. I'm on private grounds, I'm not upsetting anyone!'

The police sergeant looked even more threatening as he replied angrily, 'I don't care how you're getting on. I say you're not going to drive alone. You're not safe to go out alone. They've told me up there'—pointing to the building—'that you were given just a short time to live. I don't want you dying on the road here when I'm on duty!'

The Author was really astounded at such treatment and simply could not understand it. Admittedly he was ill, otherwise he would not have been in the wheelchair, but to expect people to accompany him every time he went out— well, that was bordering on the fantastic. There was housework to be done, all manner of things to be done, and the Author wanted to be independent. He said, 'But I am on private property.'

The detective broke in this time, saying, 'We don't care if you are on private property or not. You look as if you are going to die at any moment. We are not thinking about you, we are thinking about other people. Now you get back there and I'll follow you.' He seized the handles of the wheelchair and with extreme roughness turned the thing round, with such violence that the poor wretched Author was almost tipped out. Then, with an angry shove, he commanded, 'Get going!'

Passers-by on the roadway leaned out of their cars, grinning at the sight of a man having trouble with the police—a man in a wheelchair—but, of course, these were sightseers and when people are out sightseeing ANYTHING is a sensation. But it was always a source of astonishment to the Author that whenever he was out in an electrically-propelled chair there was always a horde of grinning apes in big American cars hooting as if it was the funniest sight imaginable. He wondered what there was so amusing in seeing an old disabled man trying to live a life without being too much trouble to other people.

But the chair was given another violent shake and the harsh command, 'Get going!' made him switch on the motor again, and go back through the car-park and up the ramp and on to the private street, the scowling detective following. At the entrance to the elevator the detective stopped and said, 'Now if you come out alone again we shall take action against you.' He started moving off to the police car which had followed, and as he did so he muttered, 'Silly old fellow, he's eighty if he's a day!'

So the Old Author got in the elevator again, went up to the ninth floor and trundled the wheelchair back into his apartment. Another door had been closed. Now apparently it was forbidden to go out alone. He would have to be like a monkey on a chain or a dog on a lead or something. Miss Cleopatra came forward and jumping on his lap said, 'Silly Unmentionables, these humans, aren't they?'

But there was work to do, there was a book to write and there were letters to answer, so the Author mentally tossed up a coin to see which he should do first. The letters won, and the first letter on top of the bunch was from a young man in Brazil, a young man of rare good sense, a young man with very, very balanced questions.

Here is the letter he wrote, and after it the letter which was a reply to him:

'Rio de Janeiro,
'Dear Dr. T. Lobsang Rampa,
  'I've already read all of your books and I'm very in-

terested to study hard everything you told us. But, like every student has some questions, I'd like you answer me the questions that I'll ask you.

'I'm sorry because I don't write (and speak) England well as I'm still learning it in the school and many of the words I saw in the dictionary. So, there are questions:

'1. If I die, I'll find many people who I've known. I'll see them like I saw them in the Earth. But, what is my real aspect whether I've already been many persons in my existence circle? How a person who I had known in a before circle, would she see me?

'2. Why just now, a ancient from Tibete, like you, came to tell us all of (everything) of the Oriental wisdom? Why just now?

'3. How could I see the Akashico Registry in the astral?

'4. What is the better position to meditate? I can't sit in the Lotus Position and I can't sit with the spine erect.

'If you think some questions shouldn't be answered, don't answer them as I'll find them in the meditation (I hope so) as I've already found most of them just thinking myself.'

'You are really a candle in the darkness and I thank you for everything.

'Thanks very much, Dr. Rampa.

'FABIO SERRA.'

'Dear Fabio Serra,

'Oh lovely! You have sent me some questions which are worthy of answering in a book I am now writing and which will have the title of "The Thirteenth Candle".

'As I propose to use your questions in this book I am going to repeat your questions and then give the answer. So, here they are:

'1. "If I die I will find many people who I have known. I will see them like I saw them on the Earth. But what is my real aspect, and not just how I look on the Earth? How would a person who knew me before recognise me?"

'Well, the answer to that is when you die you first of all leave this Earth and you go into what many religions term "Purgatory". "Purgatory" is just a place where you purge away certain things. Suppose you have been out working in the garden and have possibly got some mud on your face or on your hair (if you have any hair!). Then you decide you want to come in and have dinner and perhaps listen to the radio. So—what do you do first of all?—you visit "Purgatory". In other words, you visit a place where you can wash your hands, wash your face, and—well—purge yourself of dirt or things which should not be on you.

'Many religions make fearful pictures of "Purgatory". I prefer to regard it as a celestial bathroom where you wash your astral, so to speak, so that you may appear in front of your fellows with your territorial integrity intact. You see, when you are in the astral then you will be showing your aura, and if you have too many "dirty marks" on your aura then it will show to those who look. Purgatory, then, is a place in the astral where you are greeted by your friends and never by your enemies, because when you get to the Other Side you can only meet those with whom you are compatible. When you leave this Earth then obviously you think of yourself, you think of your appearance, as you were on this Earth, and that is how you manifest in the astral—precisely as you were on this Earth. Because the people who meet you there want to be recognised, they also will appear to you just as you knew them on Earth.

'Many times one has the same sensation on Earth. You see a person and you are sure that that person has a mole on the left side of the cheek, but another person might tell you, "Oh no, that mole was removed about a year ago." You only see, in other words, what you want to see, what you expect to see, so when you get to the Other Side you will see the people you want to see, and you will see them in the form and colour that you expect to see them in. A simple illustration—suppose you had a Negro friend, that is, the person was a Negro on Earth when you knew him. But supposing on the Other Side he was a white man; if he approached you, you wouldn't recognise him, would you? So he appears as a Negro.

'As you progress upwards then your appearance changes. In the same way you can have an illiterate savage with hair all over the place and teeth stained with various berries, etc. But if you took that illiterate savage and scrubbed him several shades lighter and gave him a shave and a haircut and fixed him up in a modern civilised suit of clothes he would look different, wouldn't he? Well, when you get to the Other Side and you progress, then you will find your appearance changing—for the better.

'The second part of that question? Well, of course, this lady whom you ask about will see you when you get to the Other Side as you are imagining yourself to be. She will see you as you were on Earth, and you will see her as she was on Earth. Otherwise (to repeat myself) you would not recognise her.

'2. "How did an ancient from Tibet, like me, come to tell Western people all about this sort of thing? Why should I come just at this time?"

'That is a fair enough question, and I will give you the answer.

'In the past there have been many people visiting Eastern areas of the world, and people from the West are material-minded. They dwell in the present, they dwell amid thoughts of money, material possessions, power and domination over others. It is part of the Western culture. Now, when they go to the East and find that many of the finest minds of the East are housed in bodies which are sick or poor or clad in rags, they cannot understand it, and so they take the ancient Teachings and, not having been born to the language, not having been born to the culture, they distort the ancient Teachings to that which they (the Westerners) think should be meant. So it is that many translators, etc., do a definite disservice to humanity in propounding fallacious statements by distorting one's true religious beliefs.

'I was prepared for a very long time. I was given the ability to understand the West while still being of the East. I was given the ability to write and to get my points clearly over to a person who is worthy of knowing the answers. I have suffered more than any person should have to suffer, but that has given me a greater insight, that has given me a greater range of expressions, of understandings, and has made my sympathetic to the Western outlook, and able to tailor my words to convey the true esoteric meaning to the Western reader.

'This is the Age of Kali, the Age of Disruption, the Age of Change when mankind truly stands at the crossroads deciding to evolve or devolve, deciding whether to go upwards or whether to sink down to the level of the chimpanzee. And in this, the Age of Kali, I have come in an attempt to give some knowledge and perhaps to weigh a decision to Western man and woman that it is best to study and climb upwards than to sit still and sink down into the slough of despond.

'In your third question you ask how you can see the Akashic Record when in the astral. To answer:

'When you enter the astral plane after having left this life you will, of course, go to the Hall of Memories and you will see everything that has happened to you, not just in the life you have just left, but in other lives that you lived before. Then you will decide, possibly with the assistance of counsellors, what you want to do to advance your evolution. You may decide that you, too, would like to help others coming from Earth. In that case, if it is definitely to your advantage to see the Akashic Record so that you may help others more genuinely, then you will be given the power to see the Akashic Record. But I must tell you that no one can see it just as a matter of curiosity.

'There are people nowadays in the West who advertise that for a fee they will travel into the astral (complete with briefcase, I suppose!) and consult the Akashic Record and come back with all the information desired. Well, of course, this is entirely untrue. They do not consult the Akashic Record, and I doubt if they ever get into the astral consciously. The only spirits they consult are the ones that come in bottles. So, I repeat, you cannot see the Akashic Record of another person unless there is some definite gain to be derived therefrom FOR THE OTHER PERSON.

'Your fourth question is, once again, a very sensible question, one which I am pleased to answer because so many people ask it, so many people are troubled. Your question is, "What is the best position to adopt for meditation? I cannot sit in the Lotus Position and I cannot sit with the spine erect?"

'Precisely! Let me tell you this; if you breathe you do not have to adopt a special position, do you? If you want to read a newspaper or a book you do not have to adopt a special position. If you want to read you take a position which is comfortable for you. Perhaps you sit in an armchair, perhaps you lie down. It doesn't matter. The more comfortable you are, the more you enjoy, the more you can absorb that which you are going to read. The same applies to meditation. Now, read this carefully ... It does not matter in the slightest degree how you sit. Sit in any way you wish. Lie down if you prefer. And if you want to lie down in a curled position, then do so. The whole purpose of resting is so that you can be free from strain. You must be free from strain and distraction if you are going to meditate successfully. So—any position that suits you suits meditation.

'There it is. You've got your answers. I hope you will find these answers of benefit to you.'

The Old Author leaned back with the satisfaction of a job well done. 'What a tremendous amount of misconception and misunderstanding there is,' he thought. Then he reached out and picked up another letter, this time all the way from Iran. One question in particular is applicable here, and that question is—What is the point of sleeping in the Lotus posture? Apart from mortifying the flesh what good does it do?

This really is a most vexed subject. It really does not matter in the slightest degree whether one sits in the Lotus Position or lies flat on one's back. The only matter is that one shall be comfortable because if one is not comfortable then there will be all manner of strains and stresses which will distract one from rest and distract one from meditation. Let us look at this a bit closer, shall we?

In the West people sit on chairs. When they go to bed they rest on a soft contraption which has springs or some device which lets portions of the anatomy sag so that if (to be unkind!) one's behind sticks out a bit too much the soft mattress or soft springs will permit one's behind to sink down in the mattress, and then the weight is more evenly distributed. The point is that in the Western world people have a system which suits them, it is THEIR system, the system to which they are born, and if a Westerner wants to sit he usually sits on some sort of platform supported on four legs and with a prop at the back to prevent him from tipping over. Almost from birth, then, he is conditioned to believe that he has to have his spine supported by something else, and so the muscles which normally would keep his spine erect become undeveloped or atrophied.

The same conditions apply in the matter of legs, their joints, etc. The Westerner is conditioned to have his legs stick out at a certain angle and bend down from the knees at a certain angle, and in any other position he is, naturally, uncomfortable.

Now let us consider the East, Japan first. In Japan, before entering a house, one discards one's footwear and then enters the house, walks into a room, and sits on the floor. The only way you can sit comfortably on the floor is cross-legged, and one variation of that cross-legged position is called the Lotus Position.

Throughout many years of development the Japanese has found that if he grabs his ankles and nearly ties his legs in a knot he is very comfortable. He is propped up on a good solid foundation, and because he has been conditioned to it from birth he finds no strain, no discomfort, no unpleasant-ness. He finds, too, that his spine is naturally erect. It just has to be because of that posture.

Take a Japanese who has never seen Western appliances before, and drop the poor wretch on to a Western chair, and he will be acutely uncomfortable. It will give him aches and pains in all the best places, and as soon as he can decently do so he will slide off the chair and flop on the floor in the accustomed position.

If one takes a Westerner and puts him in a Japanese community so that he has to sit on the floor cross-legged he suffers agony. His joints have not been conditioned to that particular position, so, to start with, he thinks he is going to split and then when the time comes to get up he usually finds he cannot. It is a delightful sight to see a fat old German who has been sitting cross-legged trying to get up. Usually he falls forward on his face and just saves himself with his hands. Then with many a hearty groan he gets his knees tucked under him somehow, and with painful creaks and gasps and guttural exclamations he gets to his feet at the same time clutching his back and wearing upon his face the most anguished of expressions.

In the Far East sitting cross-legged is an ordinary matter of everyday existence. In the West the culture developed of making money and of having material possessions. The Westerner thinks more of 'today'—thinks more of having possessions upon this Earth—and so whatever is a status symbol becomes desirable. In the days of long ago kings and emperors and pharaohs and all that type of person sat on thrones, so the ordinary person got a few lumps of wood, knocked them into shape and used them as miniature thrones or chairs. Mrs. Smith wanted a better chair than Mrs. Brown so she put some pretty cloth over it, but Mrs. Jones wanted something better; she was so bony that she was sitting on bones all the time, so she stuffed the cloth with wool and then she had the first upholstered chair.

In the Far East people were not so money-conscious, they were not so possession-conscious. They tried, instead, to store up treasure in heaven or the local equivalent of that state, and people were quite content to sit on the ground. Thus from birth they had become accustomed to sitting on the ground. Their joints are more flexible, their muscles are designed for it.

In India the Wise Man sits under the trees in Lotus Position. He has to, poor fellow, he doesn't have a chair with him and he's probably never even heard of a shooting stick!

Westerners go along and see some old fellow sitting under a tree, and they think that that is a wise man and so they confuse his posture with the acquisition of wisdom. Then you get some stupid fellow, perhaps he has seen a photograph of India or something, and he goes and writes a book all about Yoga because he has heard a friend talk about it or because he has seen something on TV (the Author has no TV; he never did subscribe to the belief in the Idiot Box).

Authors have done immeasurable harm to the real metaphysical teachings. Authors, without the actual knowledge of things, have copied the works of others and altered it a bit so that they should not actually infringe a copyright. And then again, many authors resent what appears to be a newcomer who really does know his job from first-hand experience. So authors—the ones who copy without knowing what they are doing—must take the blame for putting a completely false interpretation upon the terms 'Yoga' and similar. Many of these authors think they have to be clever and put Sri in front of their names. It is just the same as a fellow putting Mr. while living in an Eastern community. If these authors and poseurs knew anything about it they would not be so utterly stupid as to copy terms which they do not at all understand.

Many interpreters and translators have tried to take Far Eastern books and put them into English or French or German, but that is absolutely dangerous unless the translator has a remarkably sound knowledge of both languages and of the metaphysical concepts. For example, many Eastern concepts are just that—concepts. They are abstract things and they cannot be translated into concrete terms unless a person has lived in both cultures.

So we come back to the Lotus Position. The Lotus Position is just a seating posture which an Indian, or a Japanese, or a Tibetan finds convenient and comfortable. He would not feel so comfortable in a chair so he doesn't use a chair. In the same way, a Westerner cannot do so well in the Lotus Position because it is not a natural position for him.

It is well known to circus people that if one is going to have good acrobats then they must be trained actually from birth. The limbs must be trained to bend more than normal because the average Westerner has a very limited range of bone movements. The Easterner, it is usually said, is 'double-jointed'; to be more exact, the Easterner has more training in bone movement. It is highly dangerous for a Westerner of perhaps middle age to try any of the exercises which are utterly commonplace to the Easterner. It is utterly dangerous for the Westerner to try sitting in the Lotus Position after joints, etc., have become stiff.

The person who made that question all the way from Iran has another question about Ho Tai being a symbol of Good Living.

Well, of course, the Ho Tai is just one example of the Thousand Buddhas. In the Far East there are concepts instead of concrete terms. People do not worship idols, they do not worship a figure of the Buddha. The figures just act as a stimulus to certain lines of thought. For instance, a Ho Tai is a pleasant-looking old man with a fat tummy sitting in the Lotus Position. Now, that does not mean that you also have to sit in the Lotus Position. It just means that this pleasant old man with the fat tummy didn't have a chair, and if a chair had been provided he would not have used it because a chair to him would have been uncomfortable. So he sat in the position most suitable for the training which his anatomy had had—cross-legged or Lotus Position.

The Ho Tai, then, is just one of a group of figures, statues, pictures, or representations of the different phases of mankind. You can say that reaching Buddhahood is available to all, it does not matter if you are a king or a commoner, it does not matter your station in life, it does not matter if you are rich or if you are poor. You can be reaching for Buddahood whatever your station in life. The only thing to go on is—how do you live? Do you live according to the Middle Way, do you live according to the rule that you should do as you would have others do unto you? If so, then you are on the road to Buddhahood.

This Buddha business is so often misunderstood, just as is Yoga, Yogin, Lotus, etc. THE Buddha was Gautama. Gautama was his name. Perhaps it would help a bit if one refers to Christian terms; Jesus was the man. Jesus was, in another conception, 'THE Christ.' One can be Christlike but you would not be Jesuslike, would you? In the same way Buddha is a state, a rank, a status, the final result. That to which Gautama aspired and to which Gautama evolved. It is, in fact, a state of evolution, and all these different figures which many uninformed people call 'idols' are not that at all. They are merely representations, merely reminders that it doesn't matter if you are austere (the Serene Buddha) or a jovial person (the Ho Tai) one can still attain to Buddhahood provided that one does live according to the true belief which is the Middle Way, and Do to Others as You Would have Them Do to You.

The Old Author leaned back exhausted with the effort of doing work. His health had been getting steadily worse, as witness the incident with the police when yet one further door to freedom on Earth had been closed. And now he was tired of writing.

For a time he switched on the good old Eddystone short-wave receiver and listened to news around the world, from India, from China, from Japan, and from Russia. It seemed that everyone in the world was saying unkind things about everyone else. 'Ah!' he said to Miss Cleopatra. 'At least we do not have television to look at all the horrors of Western gun-shooting scenes and all that rot. I don't know why we can't have good news information on the television instead of sex, sadism, and assorted sin.'

Miss Cleopatra looked wise. She looked down and then delicately started to clean herself again although she was

118

cleaner than almost any human would be. 'Guv,' she said rather diffidently. 'Guv, haven't you forgotten something?'

The Old Author started and went into a considerable confusion of cogitation wondering what it was that he had forgotten. Why was Miss Cleopatra being so diffident? 'Well no,' he said, at last, 'no, I don't think I have forgotten anything, but if you think I have—well, just tell me and we'll see what we can do about it.'

Miss Cleopatra stood up and walked the length of the Author and then sat down on his chest in her favourite position so that she could whisper in his ear. 'Guv,' she said, 'you said earlier in this chapter about animals talking, you said about the chimpanzees. But you told me before that one should never, never quote from anybody else's book without giving the complete title and author. Didn't you forget that?'

The poor wretched Author almost blushed except that blushing was a virtue quite beyond him. Then he bowed to the Little Cat and said, 'Yes, Cleo, you are perfectly correct. I will rectify my omission now.'

Reference was made to the husband and wife team of researchers by the name of Gardner who taught a chimpanzee sign language. The information was obtained from pages 170 and 171 of the book entitled 'Body Language' by Julius Fast, published by M. Evans & Co. Inc., New York.

Miss Cleo slowly rose to her feet, yawned, turned about, and gently flicked the tip of her tail as she walked down the length of the Author again and lay across his ankles. Obviously she was highly satisfied that she had played her part in seeing that acknowledgement was given where acknowledgement was due. Having played her part she curled up comfortably and went to sleep. Every so often her whiskers flicked and twitched with the pleasantness of her pure and innocent dreams.

CHAPTER NINE

Beneath the shadowed rocks the old woman sat and sobbed her misery. Ceaselessly she rocked herself and flung herself to the unyielding ground. Her eyes were red and swollen and her furrowed cheeks were streaked with dirt which the tears had water-marked. The sunlight, as from another world, threw down strong black shadows across the entrance to her cave, shadowed bars that seemed to imprison her soul.

Beyond the mouth of the cave the Yalu River streamed endlessly on its way down from the highlands of Tibet, through India to form the sacred Ganges, and then on to the mighty seas, each drop of water like a soul going on to eternity. The waters roared and surged through close rock walls and tumbled over gorges into deep, deep pools before spilling over and rushing tumultuously on.

The path between the mountain wall and the turbulent stream was smooth, beaten hard, and level by the passage of many feet over hundreds of years. The red-brown soil would, to a Western observer, have reminded him of a chocolate bar, so brown and smooth it was. The great rocks strewn carelessly at the sides of the trail were red-brown too, with the colour which comes to rocks richly laden with ores. In a tranquil pool fed by a feeble trickle from the mountainside, there came the glitter of specks of gold. Gold from the heart of the mountains.

The tall man and the small boy rode sedately along the winding path, the path which wound so constantly close to the rock wall. The small ponies were weary, for long this day they had plodded from the small lamasery from which the sun's rays even now were glinting in the far distance towards the West. The man, in the saffron robe of a Lama, looked about him, searching for a suitable spot at which to camp.

The mouth of a cave loomed indistinctly through the screening blooms of a rhododendron tree. The Lama gestured and slid off the pony. The following pony stopped behind his fellow, and the young acolyte, unprepared, slid over the animal's head. Unhooking his pack, the Lama strode to the mouth of the cave.

The old woman was moaning in an ecstasy of misery, rocking backwards and forwards. 'What ails you, Old Mother?' asked the Lama gently. With a screech of terror the old woman jumped to her feet, then fell on her face at the sight of the Lama. Carefully he stooped and helped her to her feet. 'Old Mother,' he said, 'sit beside me and tell me what afflicts you so. Perhaps I may be able to help you.'

The young acolyte came blundering in, carrying his pack before him. Not seeing a rock ridge, he tripped over it and fell flat on his face. The old woman looked up and cackled with sudden laughter. The Lama motioned the boy away, saying, 'We will camp elsewhere, look after the ponies.' Turning again to the old woman, he said, 'Now tell me what it is that afflicts you so.'

The old woman clasped her hands together and said, 'Oh, Holy Lama, hear my tale and help me. Only you can tell me what to do.'

The Lama sat down beside her and nodded encouragingly saying, 'Yes, Old Mother, perhaps I can help but you will have to tell me of your difficulties first. But—you are not of our country are you? Did you not come from the tea country?'

The old woman nodded and replied, 'Yes, we crossed over into Tibet. We used to be on one of the tea plantations but we did not like it there, some of the Western people treated us so badly. We had to pick so much tea and always they were saying that it had too many stalks in it, so we came here and made a living by the roadside.'

The Lama looked thoughtful and said, 'But tell me, what ails you now.'

The old woman clasped and unclasped her hands, and appeared to be in an agony of indecision. Then she said, 'My husband and my two sons were living here with me. We managed quite well in helping traders to ford the river a little farther down because we know just where the crossing stones are, and we had arranged them so that we knew exactly how best the traders could cross without falling in and being swept over the gorge. But yesterday my two sons and my husband climbed up the side of the cliff. We wanted eggs and the birds were laying well.' She stopped and broke into a bout of weeping again. The Lama put an arm around her shoulder to calm her. He pressed a hand gently at the base of her neck. Immediately her sobbing ceased and she sat up resuming her tale.

'They had a good number of eggs, they had them in a little leather bag, and then—I don't know what happened exactly—my husband seemed to lose his footing, a rock rolled beneath him and he fell over. He toppled down the rockside.' She stopped to sob again, and then shaking her head as if to clear away bad memories, she resumed.

'My husband turned over as he fell and struck his head on the rocks down here. Poor fellow,' she said, 'that was always his weakest point. There was a horrible crunching and splat just like that—splat! And then a sound as if an old bundle of sticks were being stepped on.'

The Lama nodded his sympathy, and with a gesture encouraged the woman to continue.

'But up on the cliffside my sons were in great difficulty. One tried to snatch the bag of eggs from his father's hand, and as he did so he stumbled also. The second son tried to grab either the eggs or his brother—I do not know which—and he fell as well, and then there was a small rocks slide. Both boys fell, and they hit the rocks down here, splat, splat, just like that!' She cackled with an almost hysterical laugh and the Lama was some time before he could get her composed again. At last she was able to continue with her story.

'The way they hit! I shall never get it out of my mind. First there was this soggy splat, and then there was a crunching, splintering sound, so I have lost my husband and my two sons, and even the eggs were all broken up. Now I do not know what to do. Things are so difficult here.'

She stopped and sniffed and did a hoot or two full of anguish. Then she said, 'A passing trader helped me straighten them out a bit, although it was rather difficult, they were all pulpy masses, they could have been rolled up like an old garment. Probably there wasn't a bone left in their body unbroken. Then, as the trader and I stood there, a horde of vultures descended and we were horrified at how they went to work. Soon, more quickly than seemed possible, there was nothing left but the bones of my husband and my two sons, and they were shattered beyond belief.'

The Lama gently stroked the back of her neck because she was giving way again to hysteria. He gently held the back of her neck and applied a slight pressure. The woman sat upright and the colour returned to he cheeks. 'You have told me enough,' said the Lama, 'do not distress yourself.'

'No, Holy Lama, I would rather get it all off my mind if you will hear me out.'

'Very well then. Tell me whatever you wish to tell me and I will listen,' responded the Lama.

'The trader and I stood there, I do not know how long we stood there watching in horror and fright as the birds cleaned up the fragmented bones. Then—well, we couldn't leave the bones there strewn about the path, could we? We gathered up all those bones in a basket and we tipped them all in the river. They all went tumbling down over the gorge. Now I have no husband, now I have no sons, now I have nothing. You Tibetans believe in the Holy Fields; we believe in Nirvana, but I am sore distressed, I am frightened. I too would like to leave this world, I am frightened.'

The Lama sighed, and then murmured half to himself, 'Yes, everyone wants to get to the Heavenly Fields but no one wants to die. If only people could remember that although they walk through the Valley of the Shadow of Death they will experience no evil if they fear no evil.' Then he turned to the old woman and said, 'But, Old Mother, you are not going to leave this Earth yet. What is it that you fear so?'

'Living!' she answered abruptly. 'Living. What have I to live for? No man to look after me. How am I going to live, how am I going to eat, what can a woman alone do in this country, an old woman at that, an old woman who is no longer desirable to men? What can I do? I hope for death but I fear death. I have no one, I have nothing. And when I die—what then? My own religion, which is different from yours, teaches me that when I live in another life, if indeed there be another life, that I shall be reunited with my family, we shall all be together again. But how can that be, for if I live on for several years surely my family will have grown away from me, they will have grown older. I am sore distressed, I fear, and I know not what I fear. I fear to live and I fear to die, I fear what I will meet on the other side of death. It is not knowing, that is what I fear.' Impulsively she put out a hand and clasped the hand of the tall Lama. 'Can you tell me what I shall encounter beyond death?' she asked in a tremulous voice. 'Can you tell me why I should not throw myself over the gorge and die as my husband died, as my sons died? Can you tell me why I should not do this and be reunited with them? We were poor, we were humble people, but we were happy together in our own way. We never had enough to eat but we managed. And now I am an old woman alone—with nothing. Why, oh Holy Lama, should I not end my misery? Why should I not go to my family? Can you tell me that, oh Holy Lama?' She turned a beseeching look upon the Lama.

He looked at her, full of compassion, and said, 'Yes, Old Mother, it is very possible that I can bring you help by way of information. But first I doubt that you have had food or drink this day. Have you?'

She shook her head dumbly. Her eyes were brimming bloodshot tears, and her lips were trembling under the intensity of her suppressed emotion. 'We will have some tea and tsampa,' said the Lama, 'and then you will feel rather stronger so that we can talk together, and I can tell you of the things which I know to be true.' He rose to his feet and going to the mouth of the little cave called the acolyte. 'Pick up some wood and light a fire,' he said. 'First we will have tea and tsampa, and then you and I will have to talk to the Old Mother within. We will have to do our duty and try to bring her the solace of the true Religion.'

The young boy wandered off among the great rocks. There was no shortage of wood here and he wished that conditions were more like it up in the Valley of Lhasa, thousands of feet above. He wandered around picking the driest wood he could find, and collecting the most satisfactory pile.

Just a little way up on the edge of a very sharp rock he saw something which excited his avid interest. Carefully he climbed up perhaps fifty feet, and reached out a hand for the strange object which was there, a shining thing with black strands attached to it. Grasping it he recoiled in such horror that he slid down the rockface. In his hand he found he grasped the top of the skull of one of the victims. He slid down the rockface landing in a rhododendron tree which broke his fall. It also broke off many branches for which he was grateful; it saved him much work. He turned over the object in his hand, and to which he had clung despite the fall. Black hair, a bit of skin, and then the bony top of a skull. Dropping his wood he really galloped off to the side of the river and flung the thing well out towards the lip of the gorge. Perfunctorily he dipped his hands in the water to rinse them and then flicked them dry as he ran back to pick up his wood.

With an ample load he returned to a spot near the cave mouth and there he arranged a neat pile of small sticks and a little heap of tinder. Striking sparks with flint and steel, he tried to ignite the tinder which had become damp from his still wet hands.

At the cave mouth the Lama and the old woman looked out. The Lama smiled at the performance of the small acolyte, but the old woman, her stomach rumbling with hunger, said, 'Tchek, tchek, tchek,' and rushed out to the little pile of wood, her sorrows forgotten. Now she was the complete housewife about to show this young man how a fire should be lit. Quickly from her own scant supply she took dry tinder and struck a whole stream of bright sparks. Kneeling down she blew hard, and hard, and hard, and the glowing tinder suddenly burst into flames hungrily reaching out to ignite the small twigs grouped above. Beaming her satisfaction she hurried back to the cave to get a can which was already filled with water.

The young acolyte stared moodily after her, thinking why was it that women always interfered when men were doing a first-class job? Why did women always meddle and, reaping the fruits of a man's hard work, collect all the credit, all the good kharma? Irritably he kicked out at a stone and then trudged upwards between the rocks again to bring back a further load of sticks. 'No knowing how careless this old woman will be with the firewood,' he thought to himself, 'I'd better really stock up this time.'

Up near the base of the great overhanging rock he found

a bowl and a small charm box. He found a tattered scrap of rag. Looking at it he recognised it as one of the sacred devil traps. Thinking more carefully about it he remembered that some had been stolen, and then the tale came to him. 'Oh yes,' he thought, 'one of the ways they have been making money is by stealing stuff and getting it smuggled into India to be sold as souvenirs to Westerners.' He stuffed the bowl, the charm box, and the tattered scrap of cloth into the front of his robe, and spreading his arms wide he picked up the big bundle of wood and tottered precariously down the path, not being able to see where he was walking.

The old woman was busy again with the fire, and, as the poor boy had surmised, she was piling it on as if she had a whole regiment of monks to collect it for her instead of just one small boy. He dumped the pile of wood beside her, rather hoping that she would trip over it and fall into the fire and then he wouldn't have to work so hard. Then turning aside he moved towards the Lama, producing the bowl, the charm box, and the scrap of cloth. 'It is mine, it is mine, it belonged to my husband!' shrieked the old woman, jumping to her feet as quickly as if she were levitating. Rushing forward she grabbed them from the young man, and stared at them greedily. 'The only thing I have in the world now to remind me of him.' So saying she pushed the things into the bosom of her dress and turned back to the fire, tears streaming from her eyes.

The young acolyte looked gloomily at the Lama and muttered, 'Hope she doesn't get all that mess into the tsampa. I never did like messed-up tsampa.' The Lama turned away and re-entered the cave in order to conceal the mirth which was threatening to destroy his gravity.

Soon the Lama, the small acolyte, and the old woman were sitting in separate places eating the tsampa and drinking the tea, for those in Holy Orders in Tibet prefer as a rule to eat alone or only in the company of their close associates. The very sparse meal soon was finished, and the Lama, the acolyte, and the old woman cleaned their bowls with fine sand, rinsed them in the river, and put them back inside their clothes. The Lama then said, 'Come, Old Mother, let us sit by the fire and let us see what we can do to discuss and solve your problems.' He led the way back and threw a handful of sticks on the spluttering little blaze.

The young acolyte looked gloomily on, appalled at how quickly the wood was being consumed. The Lama looked up with a smile and said, 'Yes, you'd better get another load or two, we shall need some fire here. Be off with you!'

The boy turned again and wandered off in search of wood and whatever else should offer itself. The Lama and the old woman started to talk.

'Old Mother,' said the Lama, 'your religion and my religion take different forms, but all religions lead the same way Home. It does not matter what we believe, nor how we believe, so long as we do believe, for a true religion with the mental and spiritual discipline which it enjoins upon its adherents is the only salvation for our people and for yours.' He stopped and looked at her, and then resumed, 'So you had thought of killing yourself, eh? Well, that's no answer, you know. If you kill yourself, if you commit suicide, you merely add to your problems, you do not end them.' The old woman looked up at him, for he was a large tall man and she very small. She looked up at him with her hands clasped. Wringing her hands, she said, 'Oh yes, do tell me. I am ignorant, I do not understand anything, I have no knowledge at all. But yes, I had thought of killing myself by throwing myself against the gorge and becoming dashed against the rocks below even as my husband and my sons were dashed against the rocks.'

'Suicide is no answer,' said the Lama. 'We came to this Earth for the purpose of learning, for the purpose of developing our immortal soul. We came to this Earth to face certain conditions, perhaps the hardships of poverty, perhaps the great temptations which assail the rich, for let us not think that money and possessions give one ease from worries. The rich also die, the rich also become ill, the rich also suffer from worries and persecutions and from a multitude of afflictions and problems unknown to the poor. We come to this Earth and we choose our station according to the task we have to accomplish, and if we commit suicide, if we kill ourselves, we are like a shattered bowl, and if you shatter your bowl, Old Mother, how are you going to eat? If you break your flint and your steel there is no spark left with which to ignite the tinder; how then will you survive?'

The old woman nodded dumbly as if in complete agreement, and so the Lama continued:

'We come to this Earth knowing before we come what our problems will be, knowing what hardships we shall have to undergo, and if we commit suicide then we are running out on arrangements which we ourselves made for our own advancement.'

'But, Lama,' said the old woman in an agony of exasperation, 'we may know on the Other Side what we arrange, but why is it that we do not know while we are here on this Earth, and if we do not know why we are here how can we be blamed for not doing that which we say we should have to do?'

The Lama smiled down at her, and said, 'Oh what a common question that is! Everyone asks the same. We do not know usually what task we have to do upon this Earth because if we did know we should devote our whole energy to accomplishing that task no matter how much it inconvenienced others. We have to do our task and at the same time help others. We have at all times to live according to the rule, "Do as you would have others do unto you", and if in a selfish hurry to complete a given task we tread upon the rights of others, then we just make extra tasks which we have to accomplish. So it is that it is better for the majority of people not to know the task which they have to accomplish, not to know so long as they are upon the Earth.'

The discussion was interrupted by a shout from the young acolyte. 'Look! Look!' he shouted. 'Look what I have found!' He hurried into sight carrying in his hands a small golden image. The weight was considerable and he had to carry it carefully, afraid that it might drop and fall upon his feet.

The Lama rose to his feet and as he did so he happened to glance towards the old woman. Her face was a pale greenish colour, her mouth was open, and her eyes were staring wide. She looked the absolute picture of complete terror. The Lama took the figure from the boy. Turning over the image he saw on the base a mark. 'Ah!' he said. 'This is one of the figures which was taken from the small lamasery up there. Robbers broke in and this is one of the things they took.' He turned and looked at the old woman who was gibbering with fright. 'I see, Old Mother, that you knew nothing about this. I see that you had suspicions that your husband and two sons were doing something which they should not have been doing. I see that in spite of your suspicions that you were not sure, and that you had no part in this. So, fear not. You will not be punished in any way for what is the sin of another.'

He turned back to the small boy, and said, 'There should be more gold, there should be precious stones also. We will go back to where you found this, and we will cast around to see if we can find the remainder of the articles which are missing.'

The old woman stuttered and stammered and at last got out some words. 'Oh, Great and Holy Lama, I know that my husband and my two sons were doing something over at the foot of that rock,' she pointed. 'I did not know what they were doing, I did not enquire, but I saw them over there, and that is near where they fell.'

The Lama nodded, and he and the young boy walked over there together. The young acolyte said, 'But that is where I discovered this thing. It was just sticking out of the sand, so I picked it up.' Together Lama and acolyte dropped to their knees and with flat stones dug down into the sandy soil. Soon they struck something hard, and gentle riffling through the soil with their fingers dislodged a substantial leather bag in which, to their delight, were precious stones and small nuggets of gold. They dug together and ran their hands through the soil to see if anything had been missed. At last the Lama was satisfied that they had completely recovered the stolen articles. They rose to their feet and went back to the fireside where the old woman was still sitting.

'Tomorrow,' he said, 'you shall take these articles back to the lamasery. I shall give you a written message to present to the Abbot and he will give you a sum of money as a reward for the return of these articles. I shall make it clear to him in my note that you are not the guilty one. So, with the sum of money, you should be able to travel the path to your former home in Assam where possibly you have relatives or friends with whom you can live. But now let us discuss your other problems, for the things of the spirit should take precedence over the things of the flesh.'

'Holy Lama,' said the young acolyte, 'could we not have

more tea while you talk? I am very thirsty with all the hard work and all the excitement. I should like to have more tea.'

The Lama laughed, and bade the boy go to the river and get more water, and yes—they would have fresh tea.

'Old Mother,' enquired the Lama, 'what is this other matter which troubles you so? You said something about being united with your family.'

The old woman sniffed a bit in her sorrow and fright, and then said, 'Holy Lama, I have lost my husband and my sons, and even if they did steal from the temple they are still my husband and my sons, and I would like to know if I shall meet them again in another life.'

'But of course,' said the Lama. 'Much misunderstanding is caused, however, by the manner in which people on this Earth will think that things are always the same. People do not like change. They do not like anything to be different. It is different on the Other Side. Here on this Earth you had your husband and then you had your son, a baby. Later you had another baby. The babies grew up, they became small boys, they grew older and became young men, they were not the same, they grew up. It is thus on the Earth because you came to the Earth and they came to the Earth for you all to be together. But your son on this Earth may not be your son in the next life. One comes to the Earth to live a part, to carry out a certain role, to accomplish a certain task. Here you come as a woman, but on the Other Side of life you may be a man and your husband may be the female one.'

The old woman looked dazedly at the Lama. Obviously she was not taking it in at all. Obviously it was a matter beyond her comprehension. The Lama saw it, so he continued:

'In Assam when you were a girl you probably saw some of those plays about the fertility of the soil, about Mother Nature. The actors were people whom you knew, and yet when they came out to play their parts they resembled other people, they were made-up, dressed up to resemble other people, to resemble Gods and Goddesses, and you could not recognise them for whom they really were. Upon the little stage they carried out their acting and their posturing and their miming, and then they disappeared from the stage, soon after to re-appear among you as the people you well knew. They were no longer the Gods and Goddesses and the Demons of the play, they were instead men and women well known to you, your friends, your neighbours and your relatives. So it is down here upon this Earth. You are living a part, you are an actress. The ones who came as your husband and sons were actors. At the end of the play, at the end of your life, you will go back and be what you were before you came down to this stage which is the Earth, and the people you will meet on the Other Side are the people you love for you can only meet those who want to meet you and whom you want to meet. You can only meet those whom you love. You will not see your sons as small babies; you will see them as they really are. But yet you will be as a family for people come in groups, and what is a group but a family?'

CHAPTER TEN

So the end of the week came around as the end of the week always does. The Old Author heaved a sigh of relief to think there would be no mail on this day, for on a Saturday in Montreal there is no mail delivery. So while the highly paid mailmen were resting in their country cottages or going out fishing in their boats, the Old Author lay back in his bed and grumpily considered all the questions which still had to be answered. Here is a question which comes up time after time. It is:

'To me it is most important to know where I am going. Once a man is born you state that it is somewhat like a mother giving birth to a child but with the Silver Cord still remaining attached. You state that the Overself is the nine-tenths of the sub-conscious of Man or, so to speak, the man behind the scenes. All right, if this be so then let us get to the man. He starts out limited to his one-tenth, and thus runs round in the dark most of his life. The man dies (he has done his job for the Overself), the Silver Cord is severed and he is on his own. WHAT DOES THE OVERSELF GIVE HIM FOR HIS EFFORTS?'

Well, all right, let us get down to it. Yes, that is a question which can be answered. But you must remember that the Overself is the real YOU, and it is—as far as Earth terms are concerned—blind, deaf, and static, but of course only as far as this low Earth is concerned. The Overself wants to know what things are like on this Earth, it wants sensation fast because in the realm in which the Overself normally lives things move at the rate of a thousand years, or so, instead of a day. That is why in one of the Christian hymns there is that piece about a thousand years being the twinkling of an eye. But anyway, the Overself can be likened to the brain of a human. The Overself causes a human, or more than one human, to do certain things and to experience certain things, and all the sensations are relayed back to the 'brain' Overself, who then vicariously enjoys or suffers from those sensations.

We have difficulties, you know, because upon this Earth we are dealing with only three dimensions and only three dimensional terms, so how are we to get over concepts which demand perhaps nine dimensions?

You ask what sort of reward does the Overself give to the human for all the experiences which have been undergone, but there is a good question to ask in return; it is this— What reward do you give your fingers for turning a door-knob and opening a door for you? What payment do you give to your feet for conveying you along to another room in the house or to your car or for pushing you upstairs? How do you pay your eyes for sending your brain those beautiful pictures? Remember—if 'you' are the brain and you are dependent upon hands and feet and nose and eyes, all those organs are dependent upon you for their existence. If you did not exist those hands, feet, nose, and eyes would not exist either. It is completely a co-operative effort. If your fingers light a cigarette your fingers do not enjoy the smoke; possibly another part of 'you' does, but anyhow when your fingers light a cigarette other organs do not reward those fingers with kind words or expensive gifts by way of thanks. But even if 'you' wanted to reward those fingers, how would you do it? What could you give to fingers that would please them and reward them adequately? And if the real 'you' is the brain, then how can the brain, which is dependent upon those fingers, operate to reward those fingers? Do you make the left hand give a gift to the right hand and then the right hand give a reciprocal gift to the left hand, or what? Keep in mind always that the fingers are dependent on the brain for direction, the fingers are dependent upon 'you'. So there is no reward because just as the fingers and the toes are part of the whole body, so YOU are just part of the whole organism which constitutes extensions of the Overself. Here on this Earth you are just an extension in the same way as you can thrust an arm through a window and feel things in a room beyond, a room beyond the range of your sight. So there you are. You are working for yourself. Anything you do here benefits your Overself and so benefits you because you are the same

133

thing, or a part of it.

The same querist has another question which is applicable, and it is:

'If the said man must be reincarnated does he go back to the same Overself or does he get a new one? Is he sort of a permanent part of the Overself? Is man suddenly endowed with the other nine-tenths of the consciousness, or what happens?'

The answer to this—Well, your question really is, does the same body or spirit come down from the Overself? Let us suppose you get a cut on your hand. You don't get a fresh hand, do you? The hand, or rather, the cut heals because it is part of you, because it is directed by your brain to heal, it goes through the process of joining together. People are entities complete so that your Overself can direct extensions to itself to come down to Earth, and those extensions—humans—are something like the tentacles of an octopus; cut off a tentacle and it will re-grow.

My oh my! What a lot of confusion there is about this Overself business! But in an earlier part of this book the matter should have been clarified somewhat. To add possibly a little more light let us suppose that we have a big entity which has powers which we do not at present understand. This entity has the ability to think and thereby to cause extensions of itself to shoot out wherever desired—pseudopods, they are called. So our Overself, remaining in one place, has the ability to cause extensions to be sent away from the main body but still attached to it, and at the end of the extensions there is a node of consciousness which can be aware of things through touch or through sight or through sound, nodes of consciousness which merely receive on different frequencies.

Everything is vibration. There is nothing but vibration. If we think that an article is stationary, then it is merely vibrating at one particular rate. If a thing is moving, then it is vibrating at a faster rate. And even if a thing is dead it is still vibrating and actually breaking up as the body decomposes into different vibrations.

We feel a thing, no matter whether it is stationary or moving. We touch it and we feel it because it has a certain vibration which can be received and interpreted by one of our nodes attuned to that type of frequency, in other words, we are sensitive in the sense of touch.

Another article is vibrating much more rapidly. We cannot feel it with our fingers, but our ears pick up that vibration and we call it sound. It is vibrating in that range of frequencies which a higher-receiving node can receive as a high sound, an intermediate sound, or a low sound. Beyond that there is a range of frequencies which are much higher, we cannot touch them, we cannot hear them, but even more sensitive nodes termed eyes can receive those frequencies or vibrations and resolve them inside our brain into a definite pattern and so we get a picture of what the thing is.

We get much the same thing in radio. We can listen-in to the AM band which is a fairly coarse vibration or frequency, or we can go to the short-wave bands which are much faster frequencies which an AM receiver will not receive. And we can also go down (or should it be up?) to the FM frequencies, or the UHF frequencies where we can pick up television—pictures. The radio receiver for television will not pick up AM or shortwaves, just as the AM or shortwave receiver will not pick up television pictures. So there we have an everyday illustration of how we can put out extensions to receive vibrations of a special frequency. In just the same way the Overself puts out nodes—pseudopods—humans—to pick up something which the Overself wants to know about.

Horrid thought for you. Something to make your flesh creep before you go to bed; we have seen how humans make things to pick up AM radio or FM or shortwaves. Supposing your Overself regards this Earth as just AM, then the Overself can have pseudopods out in higher frequencies, eh? So sometimes you get a nightmare where the poor old Overself has got his lines crossed and you pick up impressions of bug-eyed monsters, etc. Well, there are such things, you know.

The Author picked up another letter and shuddered. He had no mirrors about, but had there been a mirror available it would have been observed that the Author turned very pale, shockingly pale. And why? How about this for a question?

'I have a question and it is this; if a puppet can enter either a male or a female body depending on what it wants

135

to learn, why is it always taken for granted that the entity which was the Dalai Lama will always incarnate as a man? Surely even this entity needs a change if it is to learn things generally rather than purely from the male viewpoint, and why can a woman never aspire to the highest level of Lamahood? In Tibet where I understand men and women are equal (or were before the Chinese arrived), why this discrimination?'

Once again a question can be partly answered by a question. Here is a question which may help; where in all history has there been a woman as a Supreme God? Can you readers tell of any single instance where a woman has been THE Supreme God? Yes, there have been Goddesses, but they have been 'inferior' to the Gods. The Dalai Lama was a God on Earth according to Tibetan belief, and so, as a God on Earth being a Goddess on Earth would not suffice. He came in male form because the things he had to do necessitated that he came in male form. But how do you know that the Overself of the Dalai Lama does not have female puppets elsewhere learning other things? As a matter of fact he did. As a matter of fact much was being learned on the female side also.

This particular Author has a screw loose about certain things. One is about the moronic press, and another is about the so-called Women's Liberation Movement. This particular Author firmly believes that women have a very important job in life, raising the future population. If women would only stop aping men—and they do definitely try to ape men and try to wear the pants, forgetting that they don't have the figure for it—then the world would be a better place. This Author believes that women are responsible for most of the troubles of the world through wanting to get out and be 'free', as they wrongly term it, instead of accepting their responsibilities as mothers. Women say they want to be equal, but are they not equal? Which is most important, a dog or a horse? They are different creatures. Men and women are different creatures, a man has never given birth without the assistance of a female, let us say, but a female can give birth without the assistance of a male by parthenogenesis. So if the Women's Lib Movement wants a boost, why not boast about that?

What greater proof of equality or even superiority can

there be than that women have the task of providing and bringing up the future race? The male co-operation in the matter only takes a few minutes, but a woman—well, she should bring up children until they are able to get on by themselves, and how she brings them up, the example that she sets them, that is how the future race will be. But now women want to beetle off to the factory where they can talk scandal, they want to be a hash-slinger, or anything except to accept the responsibility for which she is so well qualified by Nature. Women's Liberation? I think the sponsors of the Women's Liberation Movement should be slapped across the backside—hard!

The question goes on to ask why women never aspire to the highest Lamahood. Because women are irrational, that is why, because women cannot think clearly, that is why. Because women let their emotions run away with reason, that is why. If women would only stop being such asses and face up to their responsibilities, then the whole world, the whole Universe, would be a better place.

Women have the biggest task of all; women have the task of staying at home, making a home, and setting an example which future generations can follow. Are women not big enough to do their task?

Another question, 'What is the best incense to use?'

That is something which cannot be answered because it is much the same as saying, what is the best dress to wear? What is the best food to eat? One cannot say what is the best of anything until one knows for what purpose it is required. Briefly, so that this shall not be entirely negative, here are some comments; You should try different types, different brands of incense, and you should decide which is the best type FOR YOU when you are peaceful or when you are irritated or when you want to meditate. Decide which is the best for YOU on those occasions, and lay in a good supply of those types.

Incense should always be thick sticks. The thin stuff is practically useless. It is like having a musical note; if you get a thin, reedy note it merely irritates, it merely aggravates one, but if you have a good, full-bodied note, then that can be peaceful, soothing, or stumulating. So—never be fobbed off with a thin stick of incense. If you use that you are wasting your money. Sticks are to be preferred rather than powders and cones. As to where to get the stuff—well, that is another matter. But please be very sure that there is no such thing as 'Rampa Incense'. Lobsang Rampa does not endorse any particular supplier, he does not endorse any particular incense. Many people have come out with blatant advertisements about 'Rampa This' and 'Rampa That', but Lobsang Rampa has no business interests of any kind whatsoever. Sometimes there is a request for where to obtain a certain book or other items, and then a name and address is given, but these are ordinary suppliers and are entirely and absolutely unconnected with Lobsang Rampa. Other firms advertise that they are 'The Third Eye This' or 'Something That', but again it must be emphasised because of these advertisements that Lobsang Rampa does not endorse any of them, he does not favour any of them, and he does not necessarily deal with any of them.

'Oh, oh!' said the Old Author.

Miss Cleo sat up with her ears erect and her whiskers sticking straight out, looking the absolute epitome of alertness and interrogation. The Old Author smiled at her and said, 'Hi Clee, listen to this. We've got a letter here from a pressman. He is a Press reporter with the So-and-So, So-and-So newspaper in the City of So-and-So and Something-Else. He is very cross, Clee, because he's read one of the Rampa books referring to the cowardly men of the Press. He thinks the Press are God-inspired, the Press have a right to write anything they want about people because they are doing holy work. Holy work, do you hear that, Clee?' asked the Old Author. 'This pressman asks for a definite statement from Lobsang Rampa of how the Press do any harm. The Press, he says, do only good.'

The Press could be an instrument of tremendous good, but so could television. But both pander to the lowest emotions of mankind—sadism, sensuality, superstition, and assorted sinfulness. The big complaint against the Press is that they burst into print without being sure of their facts. The Press get hold of some rumour and immediately they print it as absolute fact, and if the rumour is good then the Press distort it because sensationalism and sadism seem to sell more successfully than anything good.

The Press talk about their freedom—the freedom of the Press—but how about freedom for individuals? If the Press are to have freedom to write whatever they want to write, then the people about whom they write should also be afforded equal space in the columns of the papers to refute the lies which the Press have written. Instead of that, if any attempt at refutation is made, the Press take sentences out of context and write up a thing which becomes perfectly damning as it appears to emanate from the person concerned but is actually just a mish-mash of statements taken haphazardly, or perhaps not haphazardly; perhaps with that devilish cunning which only Presss reporters seem to possess.

Many people who are not in a position to defend themselves are attacked by the Press. Charlie Chaplin, for example, has been attacked and attacked and attacked most unfairly by the Press. Prince Philip is another; he also has been attacked and has no means of defending himself. What about the freedom of the Press? How about the freedom of the people who are attacked?

The Press cause wars and race hatred. The Press print only that which is sensational and which is calculated to stir up trouble. Without the Press there would probably have been no war in Viet Nam. There would have been no war in Korea. Without the Press causing race hatred there would not be so much trouble between different colours of humans, and now—the Government of the United States is having grave trouble because the Press, against the wishes of the Government, have burst into print with matters which should be kept quiet.

Every person has something which he wants to keep private. Every person has something which, while perfectly all right within the family, might look a bit 'off' to an outsider who did not know the exact facts and circumstances. The same appears to be the case with these Pentagon papers which the Press are now purveying as sensational things. It is causing trouble in Canada, England, France, and many other countries—just because the Press people want a few extra cents for their newspapers. In this Author's opinion the Press is the most evil force which has ever existed upon this world; in this Author's opinion unless the Press be checked and controlled and censored the Press will eventually control the world and lead to Communism.

The Old Author lay back and smiled at Miss Cleopatra as he said, 'Well, Clee, I wonder if that awful fellow, that Press reporter with the ... newspaper in the city of ... will take this to heart. I hope so. It could be one step towards salvation for him to leave his job with the Press and take something decent elsewhere.'

But let us turn aside from the Press and deal with some more questions. They are never-ending, aren't they? But it shows that there is a great need for some source whereby the questions may be answered, even partially.

Here, from England, are some questions and the answers:

1. 'Is it wrong to have an animal "put to sleep" when it is suffering and is perhaps incurably ill?'

As a Buddhist one should not take life, but there are certain things which are greater than any of the established religions, whether it be Buddhism, Christianity, Judaism, Hinduism, or anything else, and this is what one might term a duty to the Overself. In this Author's opinion it is definitely kinder to the animal to have it painlessly killed if according to the present state of veterinary knowledge it is incurable.

If an animal is suffering from such an illness that veterinary science cannot alleviate its suffering, then it is better to get a Veterinarian to destroy it as painlessly and as quickly as can be. That is kind. This particular Author is very, very experienced in the matter of pain, having had more than his fair share, and as such he would have welcomed another stronger force which could put him out of his pain permanently.

Suicide is something quite different. Suicide is wrong. Suicide is very, very wrong indeed and those who are contemplating suicide truly have the balance of their mind disturbed by sorrow, pain, or by other circumstances which affect their judgement. Euthanasia would not be suicide because euthanasia would use the judgement of mature minds who were not directly involved and as such were not swayed by distressing emotions, who were not swayed by self-pity or by pain. Suicide, according to this Author's belief, is irrevocably wrong and should never be resorted to.

If an animal is ill it should be put out of its misery. If a human is ill, incurably so, and of an advanced age where he is a burden to others, then there should be a form of euthanasia in which the matter could be discussed with those who have no personal interest.

This next question has bearing on the one above because the question is, 'Would it be possible to have the animal sent back during a human's life?'

The answer is, of course, 'Yes,' if it were to the animal's benefit. So that if—this, of course, is just by way of a purely hypothetical example and must not be taken too seriously—an animal is put out of his misery without having done his job, then it is possible that that same animal could elect to come back to the same family as a young kitten or a young puppy, and live out that period of time of which it had been deprived by being 'put to sleep' as an alleviant of suffering. It does happen. But, of course, if an animal is on the Other Side of life and if the 'owner' can do astral travel, then they can meet IF THEY BOTH DESIRE IT.

The next question—'Does the astral form have an aura, or only the physical?'

The physical form, the basic form down here on Earth, has an etheric and an aura. Both are just reflections of the life form within. Many people cannot see the aura—most people cannot see the aura—because they are so used to it in the same way that most people cannot see the air in which they live; all they can see is the smog, and there is plenty of that to see nowadays.

In the astral world the aura is much brighter around astral figures, and the greater the degree of evolution of an astral figure the more brightly the aura flashes, scintillates, and undulates. So the answer is—Yes, very definitely there is an aura around astral figures. But just as on the Earth some people cannot see the aura, so there are those in the lower astral who cannot see the astral aura. That is a matter which improves as the 'nonseer's' evolution increases.

This person in England asks some sensible questions! It is from a very intelligent English woman (do you get that, Reader? I am praising a woman!). 'Would it be permissible,' asks the question, 'to use information gained from the Akashic record to write true histories of ancient civilisations and true biographies of famous people?'

No, because you would not be believed. Ancient history resembles printed history only by accident. History is written, or re-written, or erased according to the whim of dictators, etc. A fairly modern-day example is the history of Nazi Germany. It is fairly common knowledge that history was altered a bit so that Hitler appeared to be something different from what he really was. It is fairly common knowledge also that Russian history has been altered to suit the Communist dictators. So the whole point is, if you wrote the truth from the Akashic Record you would find that it was not believed because it diverged so greatly from the official history of the country concerned.

In the matter of biographies, etc.—well, if one writes the truth one cannot often get it published, and if it is published there is usually an awful commotion after because some pressman turns up a faint rumour and he breathes heavily on the flame until he makes a roaring furnace which consumes the truth. If you want the real truth you will have to wait until you go into the astral to live!

I say, Miss C., you've got some good questions! I am going to use another of yours. You say, 'Is abortion always wrong?'

I say, no, it is often very much better to have an abortion rather than to bring into an already over-populated world some poor little wretch who will not be wanted and who may have an extremely difficult time through no fault of his own. After all, why should he be penalised for a few moments of carelessness on the part of the parents? If there is an early abortion, then an entity has not yet taken possession of the body.

By the way, Reader who complained of too many 'I's', surely by the time I have reached this stage of the book I can cease to be an Old Author and can be an Old Man instead, because I assure you I am not an 'Old Woman'. Anyway, in my books I try to keep the personal touch because we are all friends together, aren't we? We are not stuffed ducks standing on pedestals. Get yourself on a pedestal and you can soon get knocked off.

Here is another of our soul questions. It is, 'If the soul leaves a person who has become like a cabbage should the medical profession keep all the cabbages alive by purely mechanical means?'

A personal opinion is—No. When a person gets to such a stage that the entity is no longer there and life is being sustained entirely by mechanical means, then it is wrong and foolish to sustain that life. Under such conditions mechanical means should be stopped and the body should be allowed to die. This is the kindest method. One hears so much nowadays of absolutely incurable people who are longing to die, who are being kept alive with whacking great tubes stuck in them and all sorts of devilish electronic devices—well, that is not life; that is living death. Why not let them 'go home'?

'With the population explosion there is increased pressure on the wild-life and wild places of the world—will these survive or will Man ruin his environment forever?'

Many animals, birds, and fish, will die and their species will be eliminated for all time from this Earth. Mankind is insatiable and voracious. Mankind has no thought for the people of the wilds, but only for putting a few more bucks in his pocket. As this is being written there is a scheme here in the Province of Quebec whereby millions of acres of land is going to be denuded of its trees to go into the papermaking industry because from some of these paper products newspapers are printed, artificial leather is made, and many other products which Man now finds indispensable to his existence for some reason.

With the felling of the trees there will be no insects, no birds; no places for the birds to nest, no food for them, and so they will starve. Animals without shelter and without food will starve also.

Man is committing suicide and ruining his world fast. With the removal of the trees there will be different thermo currents. The temperature of the trees caused air to rise and rain to fall, so without the trees there will be a climatic change. It could become a desert area in Quebec where the trees are being felled by the millions.

The roots of trees reach out into the soil and keep it together in a solid mass. When the trees are felled and the roots pulled up there will be nothing holding the soil together, so the winds will come and blow the light soil into the air leaving desert areas reminiscent of the Dust Bowl of America.

Mankind is ruining his world because of his quite insatiable money-grabbing. If people would only live more naturally without some of theses synthetic compounds then they would be happier. As things are now, with all the developments of mankind, there is more and more pollution of the air and of the water and the soul, and soon there will come the point of no return when the earth will become barren and uninhabitable. Many people in high places out of this Earth, out of this world, are working hard to influence mankind so that this insensate destruction of the wild places of life shall be stopped, and so that Nature shall be afforded an opportunity of restoring the ecology to that which is most suitable for Man's continuance and for Man's evolution.

But—what is this? A large brown envelope inside of which there was a folded newspaper and a letter. The Old Author looked at the paper and put it aside quickly as it was a French language newspaper and he did not read French. The letter was in English. It said that the newspaper had an article by a man who was saying that Lobsang Rampa was ill and had retired and that he (the subject of the article) had now taken over as Lobsang Rampa's successor. The writer of the letter wanted to know who was this successor to Lobsang Rampa? Was it true?

There have been many people who claim to be Lobsang Rampa. But about this newspaper article first, No, I have no successors. No, I have no disciples, no students. I have no one who is my 'heir'. When I die and leave this Earth I shall have done all that I have tried to do, and if anyone sets up as my successor, my heir, my representative, then he is indeed definitely a fake. Let me repeat once again in capital letters—I HAVE NO SUCCESSORS. THERE IS NO ONE TO WHOM I HAVE DELEGATED ANY 'AUTHORITY'.

One of the awful things about being an author who is fairly well known is the number of people who go about and claim that they are that author. For instance, not long ago I had a letter from an air hostess who said how glad she was to meet me on a recent air flight, but where was the set of autographed books which I had promised her? I am confined to a wheelchair or to a bed. All my flights are made in the astral without air hostesses. There have been quite a number of instances when people have passed themselves off as me. Sometimes they have been offensive to other people, and other people have written to me complaining of my attitude. Sad, eh? Possibly this sort of thing could be stopped if everyone had identity cards because I have had bills charged to me and all sorts of things without even knowing the first thing about it. So, you have been warned. You should know what I look like by now, although I think sometimes the pictures on the covers of my books are painted by a blind man in complete darkness.

'Now, Lobsang Rampa, I would like your opinion in general about healing. Is it wise of a person living in the twentieth century to get herself involved in this? I mean, doctors are so clever nowadays, they can do almost anything, so are we needed? Then take the ordinary man today, he does not know what you are talking about if you tell him you can cure a headache quickly instead of him taking a lot of pills. He will tell you that you are just right for a mental home. So, I would like to hear from you. Is it wise to use this healing ability?'

No, it is definitely unwise to use any so-called healing ability unless one has definite medical knowledge. It is possible to have a person suffering from a very dread disease, and it is perfectly possible by hypnotism to disguise the symptoms. But although one can disguise them, one is not curing the illness, and if the person feels ill or becomes even more ill and then goes to a doctor, well—the symptoms have been disguised so what can the poor unfortunate doctor do? Had it not been for the disguised symptoms, the doctor possibly could have located the precise disease and cured it.

Unless one has definite medical knowledge and is working with the co-operation of a registered medical practitioner one should never, never go in for these healing things because they can be lethal. The same goes for this prayer stunt. When a whole bunch of people get together to pray about a certain thing, unless they know the precise condition and circumstances they may invoke the law of reversed effort and make things a whole lot worse than they were before. So, the best motto to adopt is, 'Leave well alone.'

Dear, dear, a whole bunch about the same sort of thing! All right, let's have a second on this, shall we? This next question is, 'Why is it that, say you have two people who suffer from the same type of illness, that one can be cured instantly and the other does not respond at all?'

The answer is as stated above, that one person is so hypnotised that the symptoms have been disguised and you think the person is cured instantly, while the second person is not so susceptible to hypnotic suggestions and so there is no change. Note, 'hypnotic suggestions' because healing, faith healing, etc., is basically of a hypnotic nature.

Question—'Why is it that when I heal other people my hands become hot, but when I give myself healing they become ice cold?'

Answer—When you are healing, or trying to heal, another person you are giving a hypnotic suggestion that he gets better, but you are also giving excess prana which you have available, so the passage of this prana makes your hands become hot. Naturally you cannot give your own prana to yourself because you already have it, and so you are, in effect, invoking the law of reversed effort and merely depleting your own energy and so your hands become cold.

This healing power, so-called, is basically hypnotic and being able to put over an acceptable suggestion to a susceptible person. But healing power is also possessing a large amount of etheric energy which we will call prana, and if you have this energy you may, if you are versed in such things, be able to convey it to another person. It is like having a car which is stuck on a cold morning because the battery is low. The car won't run because the battery is too low to turn over the starting motor, so then another car comes along and the driver gets out and he connects his battery to the discharged battery of the stalled car. Then there is a large flow of energy and the stalled car starts right away. That should give you an idea of how this transference of energy takes place.

CHAPTER ELEVEN

We seem to be quite international. We have had questions so far from Africa, India, Iran, England, so let's get one from nearer home, one from Quebec. The question is about retarded children. 'What purpose does a child have who is born retarded, or even crippled or blind? I know that nothing is ever in vain, but I do not see the reason for all the retarded children we have in our society. I might sound cruel, but how can these poor souls learn anything? Are they not better off dead?'

Answer—Some of these retarded children are born in their retarded condition because before coming to the Earth they definitely chose that sort of life to gain that sort of experience. After all, how can you be acquainted with the sensations of a retarded child if you have never been one? And if you have never been a retarded child and recovered, how can you help retarded chidren?

Other retarded children are cases which could be greatly improved; they may be caused by carelessness at birth or simply by bad training, often by elderly parents. But invariably most of the latter class have a 'poor connection' with the Overself, and thus the messages are not properly relayed. Of course there are in the world many people who should be sent 'Home' just as one sends an animal 'Home' when it is obviously incurable, but it is one of those things which we just cannot do because public opinion is not yet in favour of it. In theory it is the best thing to kill a person who is mentally retarded—in theory. In actuality it would be impossible to distinguish between those who were incurable for the purpose of learning, and those who actually are learning nothing but bitterness. There is a further point, and it is this; the person who is incurable today and so a candidate for euthanasia might be cured tomorrow or next week by the advancing sciences.

A nice question, this, one which I am sure you will like. It is—'To what extent should one be forgiving? The Bible says "An eye for an eye and a tooth for a tooth," but this is inhuman. The man Jesus said to forgive seventy times seven, yet this is impossible in today's life. How much tolerance should one give?'

Well, this is an answer which might make certain old ladies of either sex blush, but I have a rough rule for how much one should take. I know all about 'turning the other cheek', but really, you know, we have only four cheeks, two in front and two behind. When all four have been slapped then it is time to slap back—much harder—and stop the nonsense once and for all, because to continually sit back meek and mild and take all the abuse which is hurled at one is just to prove oneself a ninny and a weakling and not worthy of any consideration at all. We should consider, are we man or mouse? If we are mouse, then squeak to your heart's delight but run back into the woodwork out of the way. If you are a man—or mankind—then if people go beyond certain limits it is foolish to tolerate any more.

'Dr. Rampa,' the letter started, 'you can look into the Akashic Record, you know what is going on. Tell me, what was the truth about the Shakespeare affair? Did Shakespeare write his books, or what?'

Yes, for those who know how and who know how not to abuse it, the Akashic Record is available—for special purposes. But it doesn't really matter who Shakespeare was or why there is all the mystery, but here are some absolute facts.

The poor farmer's boy who was later to be known as Shakespeare, had a very great attribute. He had a 'frequency' which was entirely compatible with an entity who needed to come to the Earth to do a special task, so the boy who was to be known as Shakespeare was watched very carefully, watched as the careful gardener watches the blooming of a rare and precious plant. At the appropriate moment arrangements were made whereby the entity then inhabiting the body of the person who was to be known as Shakespeare, the author, was released from what to him had become tiresome bondage. He didn't like a life of poverty, a life of hardship, and so it was easy to arrange that the entity controlling Shakespeare left—relinquished his control—and passed on elsewhere.

The entity who had this special task to do and who for some considerable time had been seeking a suitable vehicle because it is so wasteful for such high entities to have to come down and be reborn and risk losing much knowledge through the traumatic experience of birth, the entity looked for a suitable grown host, and when the time was ripe the body was vacated by one and instantaneously re-occupied by the other.

Now there was a giant intellect in the body of the poor peasant, a giant intellect which had some considerable difficulty in adjusting to the confined space, in adjusting to the limited convolutions of the brain. And so for a little time there was a period of stasis during which no creative work was done. Then the giant entity controlling the peasant body set forth to London, set forth to explore, to become accustomed to the new body, and to overcome its gaucheries.

With the passage of time, and as increasing familiarity had been acquired over the body and over the brain, the entity began its task, writing immortal classics. But the writings were obviously impossible to an author of that body's apparent upbringing. So it is throughout the years there have been doubts, scepticisms, and wild surmises about who was Shakespeare, who wrote the works of Shakespeare.

The answer? The entity who took over the body of Shakespeare wrote those works because that was his task, and having accomplished his task he departed leaving behind him what to many is an enigma, a problem without solution. Yet if mankind would only listen to others who have had similar experiences, they too would be able to consult the Akashic Record and know something of the true marvels amid which we live.

Here is another question which may be of some interest. It is, 'When you say patience is needed to achieve astral travel, do you mean, weeks, months, or years? Or does the period vary widely according to the person concerned, the amount of time they have been practising, and the individual latent ability?'

Actually astral travel is done by all of us. Most people are unconscious of it, and when they have an experience which they dimly remember in the morning they put it down as a dream or imagination.

Astral travelling, or rather, learning to astral travel, is much the same as learning to ride a bicycle. Really it sounds quite impossible that anyone should ever learn to ride on two wheels, and as for those unicycle things——! Well, people can learn to ride a bicycle or a unicycle. People can learn to walk a tightrope, and there is no set time for how long it will take one to become proficient. It is only a knack. If you believe you can ride a cycle, then you can ride a cycle. If you believe you can walk a tightrope or a slack rope either, then you can do so. It is the same with astral travel. It is not possible to set out a list of exercises on how you start to astral travel. How would you tell a person the manner in which he should learn to ride a bicycle? How would you tell a person how he would learn to use roller skates? Besides the obvious one of tying a cushion to his posterior, that is. And again, how would you teach a person how to breathe so that he could live? Breathing is a natural thing, we just do it. We are not always conscious of doing it, are we? We are only conscious of breathing when there is some difficulty. We are not conscious of astral travelling, either, most of us, but it is just as easy as breathing, just as easy as riding a bicycle.

The main thing is that you should decide that you are going to astral travel *consciously*. The emphasis is on the word 'consciously'. Unfortunately the word 'imagination' has a bad name. People think that to imagine a thing is to pretend something which does not exist. Perhaps we should say 'visualise' instead. So to start astral travel you should go to bed—alone, of course, and in a room alone also. You should rest in any position whatever so long as it is comfortable. If you could stand on your head that would be quite all right if you found it comfortable. But if you want to lie on your back, on your side, on your front, so long as it is comfortable, that is all you need do. If you find it comfortable then it is all you need.

So—lying down comfortably, make sure that your breathing is complete, that is, slow, and deep, and even, naturally, comfortably, not forced. Lie like that for a few moments, collecting your thoughts. Then with the light out visualise yourself as a body within a body, visualise you are in a body withdrawing from your outer body in much the same way as you would withdraw your hand from the glove which encompassed it.

Form a mental picture of your body just as you are lying on the bed. Do you have pyjamas on? Then visualise them, even to the stripes or patterns or flowers. Do you have a nightdress? Visualise that precisely as it is. Do you have pretty little bows and laces round the neck? Well be sure you visualise them. Or are you one of those hardy souls who sleeps like a peeled banana? Well, visualise yourself just as you are. And then go on with your visualisation to imagine (sorry! VISUALISE) your astral form to be absolutely identical with the outer form. Visualise this body sliding out of the flesh body and rising up so that it is about an inch or two above the flesh body. Hold it there, just concentrate on visualising what it is like. If you are a girl you will have long hair, but that is a mistake because boys, too, seem to have long hair nowadays. But, anyway, if you have long hair visualise it hanging down. Is it touching the face of the flesh body? Then push it up a few inches. Visualise that body as a solid creation. Look at it from the top, from the ends, and from underneath so that you get a complete picture, a solid picture of it. Then let yourself feel satisfaction. You are out of the body. Do you feel the astral body swaying up and down slightly? Be careful, if it sways too much you will have a dreadful feeling of falling, and then you will slam back into your flesh body again with a horrid 'bonk' which will jerk you back to being just in bed.

Be satisfied for the moment thinking of your body, your astral body, floating a little way just above your flesh body. Then gradually visualise the astral body sinking back inside the flesh body just as you would slide your hand into a glove.

Try that for a night or two until you can hold the visualisation strongly, and when you can do that go further.

You have got out of your body. You are floating just above your flesh body. Think—where do you want to go? Do you want to go and see Dr. Armand Legge, the doctor who gave you such a bad medical report, or something? All right, you know what he is like. Think of him, think of yourself travelling, think of yourself arriving. If you can do it like this you can just tickle him on the back of his neck. He will become frightfully uncomfortable! But perhaps it's a little unkind to tell you of a trick like that.

Do you want to think of your girl friend? Well, you can go and see your girl friend, too, if you want to. But remember if you have the wrong thoughts in your mind about what you are going to see you will find that until you've got an awful lot of practice you'll end up back in your body with a hearty slap. What happens is this; you get out of your body, you think you will go and see some girl friend or someone whom you would like to have as a girl friend. You know it's her bath time and you want to see if she has any moles on her birthday suit. You get there, but her aura detects your presence and alerts her subconscious. Her consciousness may feel uneasy, she may keep looking over her shoulder or something, she may wonder if the landlord is peeping through the keyhole. She won't see you, but her aura will sense you and the subconscious will rise and give you such a bonk that you will forget all that you have seen and you will be chased back to your body with more of a shock than you thought possible. Only when your thoughts are pure can you intrude on a person's privacy like this, and to those people who write in and ask how they can peep at their girl-friends at the wrong time—well, the answer is, for your own sake don't. You will get pretty rough treatment.

Practice this visualisation. It is an easy thing indeed. When you can visualise it, then you can do it, so how long it is going to take depends upon you, upon how quickly you can realise the truth. The truth is that you DO astral travel, but because of civilised conditioning, etc., you do not always realise it, you do not always remember it, and when you do remember it most times you pass it off as imagination, a dream, or as wishful thinking. As soon as you accept the reality of astral travel then you can sincerely visualise astral travel. And when you can sincerely visual astral travel, then, believe me, you can do it because it is far more simple than getting up off a chair, it is far more simple than picking up a book. Astral travel is basic, it is part of a living person's birthright, no matter whether it be a horse, a monkey, a human, or a cat—every one does astral travel. But how quickly you do it consciously—that depends on you.

Curiouser and curiouser; the very next question is: 'You say that in the astral everything shimmers, but to me everything shimmers always. Is it because I wear glasses?'

When you are in the astral everything shimmers because it is full of life, full of vitality. If you are doing it properly you can see little speckles of light around you. You see as if everything was in a shaft of sunlight. No doubt you have been on some grimy railroad station and had a shaft of sunlight peer in through a murky window. In the shaft of sunlight you have seen little specks floating about. Well, in the astral everything is like that, you are in perpetual sunlight, and everything shimmers with the vitality of life. It is the opposite of being in smog. In the astral, by the way, bad sight does not matter. It does not matter if you are blind. In the astral you have all your senses. You can hear and see, you can smell, and you can feel. A hundred per cent efficiency every time. So why not try astral travel? It is easy and it is natural. And, finally, astral travel is utterly, utterly safe. You cannot get hurt, and so long as you are not afraid no harm of any kind can ever happen to you. If you are afraid, well you are just wasting energy. There is nothing to it except that. The only thing is, if you are afraid you are dissipating your energy needlessly, and—you are slowing down your vibrations so much that you are making it difficult to stay in the astral in the same way that an aeroplane that loses its forward speed sinks. You don't want to sink, do you? All right then, don't be afraid. There is nothing of which to be afraid!

So the questions come rolling in ad infinitum, add two and two together. The old typewriter goes clacking away and the pages come churning out—not churning out really because everything is thought out, but with a bit of practice typing comes fast. So the pages come out anyway, which means as there are more and more pages there is less and less room for further questions. So let us answer just one more question in this chapter. Here is a good one:

'You tell us that when we are on Earth we are only one-tenth conscious, but from what we read in your books it does appear that we are less conscious than are beings who inhabit other planets; the Gardeners of the Earth, as one example, either are in possession of one hundred per cent awareness or they must have greater power than Earth people, or is it that in their third dimensional state they could be more than one-tenth conscious? Their intellect and technical knowledge seem to be so far beyond ours, not only their intellect but their compassion and understanding. Can you explain this, please?'

Yes, sure, nothing to it. On this Earth we are upon one of the most measly of little dust spots in the Universe. You see, there are more planets, more worlds, than there are grains of sand upon all the sea-shores of the Earth, and you can throw in for good measure all the sand on the seabed too, because the number of universes is beyond human comprehension. If you get a bit of dirt beneath your nail and you look at it all beneath a microscope you find there are thousands of bits of dirt. But then think of all the stuff on the surface of your body, think also that no matter how this 'dirt' appears to you, yet still it is formed of the basic carbon molecule. So, piece of dirt beneath a nail, how are you going to imagine how many molecules—how many worlds—there are in one human body? And having decided upon that, how about all the other human bodies, the animal bodies, the bodies on other worlds, etc.

Upon this world we are one-tenth conscious, but upon other worlds people may be several more tenths conscious. But if they were even one-twentieth conscious they could still be far more intelligent than the people of Earth.

The Gardeners of the Earth are not just three-dimensional people living somewhere out there in space ready to slap down an intruding astronaut or cosmonaut. They are in a different dimension also, and of course their technical abilities are so far above that of humans that humans to them would be like a particularly scruffy microbe sitting on a particularly scruffy piece of dirt.

The big difficulty is that upon this Earth we have to live and deal with three dimensional terms, so how is one to describe things which happen perhaps in nine or more dimensions?

So, to answer the question—yes, upon this Earth we are only one-tenth conscious. And, yes, we are less conscious than are beings who inhabit superior planets, even if, by chance, they also should be only one-tenth conscious.

Yes, the Gardeners of the Earth are much more conscious, and they are also much more conscious in many more dimensions. They have worked their way up from what we are now, and yet above them there are higher beings and to them the Gardeners of the Earth are just as we appear to the Gardeners of the Earth. But if we adopt the correct law, and that law is that we should do that which we would have others do unto us, then we too can climb our way up to the state of the Gardeners of the Earth and from thence onwards. The best way to explain it is to take the R.A.F. motto, 'Through Hardship to the Stars.'

CHAPTER TWELVE

Henrietta Bunn glowered gloomily as she looked at her friend. 'Can't understand this author,' she complained, 'here am I trying to study his books and there is no Index. How does he expect one to find a thing again—read all the books?' Her breath trailed off into a series of muttered fulminations as she flipped the pages as well as her lid.

Her friend, Freda Prizner, smiled indulgently, 'Well, you know, Hen,' she replied, 'I read his books for pleasure. The thought of STUDY turns me off and I want someone to Turn me On!' She sighed and added, 'But you got something there, girl, all books should have indexes so you can look up what you want to avoid.'

The poor wretched Author groaned as he wriggled in discomfort on his hard steel bed. What DO people want? he wondered. First, it is a 'sin' to use too many I's—and after all, am I not entitled to an I or two more than average? There is 'The Third Eye', you know! But now Readers (bless their hearts—one to each Reader!) want an Index!!! The Old Author felt his pangs and pains increase at the mere thought.

Deep in the Heart of the United States where the Buffaloes no longer roam (the Elks having taken over instead) a most brilliant and talented woman was hard at work. With one husband—she says it is enough!—and two children—she says it is too many as they are boys!—to look after, she STILL found time to compile An Index. Out of the blue it came, well no, this is a TRUE book. Out of a mailman's mail sack it came. A package. The Old Author's fumbling fingers easily unwrapped the parcel because it had already been opened by Canada Customs (a very BAD custom they have). Inside—INSIDE—yes, you guessed it. THERE was An Index.

Mrs. Maria Pien is a brilliant woman, talented and capable. Yet no one is perfect; even she has a fault. Her writing is minute, and the Old Author has rapidly failing sight. So to read Mrs. Pien's writing a STRONG magnifying glass is used. She missed her vocation; her natural work should be to write books on the head of a pin.

Thank you, Mrs. Pien, for your greatly-appreciated work. Thank YOU, Miss Sekeeta Siamese Pien, for keeping her up to it.

In the interest of space, the initials of the title are used, thus:

The Third Eye	= TE
Doctor from Lhasa	= DFL
The Rampa Story	= RS
Cave of the Ancients	= CA
Living with the Lama	= LWL
You—Forever	= YF
Wisdom of the Ancients	= WA
The Saffron Robe	= SR
Chapters of Life	= ChL
Beyond the Tenth	= BT
Feeding the Flame	= FTF
The Hermit	= TH
The Thirteenth Candle	= TC

INDEX

Abortion: TC 142
Admiral: TH 63, 78
Admiral's Speech: TH 87, 91
Advice: FTF 157
Age of Kali: ChL 21, 86, 177; BT 104, 108; WA 11; FTF 120, TC 112
Akashic Record: RS 158; CA 94; YF 108, 137; ChL 131; BT 37, 84, 123, 129; TH 92; TC 113, 141–2
Alcoholism: DFL 54; CA 182; YF 88, 197; BT 137; FTF 164
Animals: RS 38; YF 218; ChL 70; BT 27; FTF 34, 38, 134, 149, 152; TH 72, 139, 146
Animal Soul: BT 27; FTF 34, 134
Animal Death (destroy): FTF 127; TC 140–1
Anti-Gravity: FTF 146–7; TH 86
Anti-Matter: ChL 50, 54; TC 82
Arc of Space: TH 139, 140, 146
Assassinations: BT 109
Asteroid Belt: TH 147
Asthma: ChL 189; BT 139
Astral Body: FTF 136; YF Less. 8; TC 141
Astral Telephone: YF 188, 191; FTF 23, 67; TC 13–14, 82
Astral Travel: TE 105, 167; DFL 25, 86; RS 30, 32; CA 67; YF Less. 8, 9, 10, 11; Page 118; YF 120, 123; WA 15; SR 100; ChL 110, 126, 147, 169; BT 17, 32, 38, 120, 126, 129; FTF 74, 80, 105, 116, 131; TH 70, 104; TC 10, 12, 16, 150
Astral Trip (Zhoro): RS 32
Astral Worlds: ChL 126; BT 17, 22; FTF 36, 131, 134; TC 110–11, 130
Astrology: TE 37, 70, 109; ChL 184; BT 133
Atlantis: FTF 142, 147; TH 141
Atmosphere: TH 136
Atoms: YF Less. 1; TH 88
Atomic Power: TH 74, 139
Atomic Weapons: DFL 166; CA 95; FTF 138; TH 141
Aura: TE 74, 102, 149; DFL 64, 67; RS 21; CA 144, 150, 164; YF 30, 52; WA 16; SR 205; ChL 191; BT 149; FTF 182, 185; TH 90; TC 27, 111, 141
Auric Machine (Photog.): DFL 66; RS 22, 26; CA 161, 165; BT 149
Auric Sheath: YF 45
Autohypnotism: YF Less. 28–29; WA 56
Avatar: YF 184

Bad Habits: YF 213
Beginning of Times: DFL 159; CA 84, 91

Beliefs: TE 100
Bible: ChL 23, 207; BT 85; FTF 34; TH 154
Birth Control: CA 184
Birth of Earth: TH 123, 133, 134
Birth of Worlds: TH 23
Blindness: TH 9, 15, 31, 52, 59
Body: TH 31
Body Sounds: TE 135; TH 47; TC 28
Books: CA 74, 134, 170; ChL 196; TC 13
Brainwashing: DFL 92
Brain Waves: YF 153, 165
Breathing: TE 168; DFL 196; YF 151, 207; WA 21, 133; TC 74, 87, 89, 91
Buddhism: SR 22; YF 218; WA 22; FTF 92
Buddha: TC 118

Calendar: TE 108
Calm: YF 166, 168
Cats: TE 148; RS 76; CA 123; SR 15, 89, 174; LWL 87, 92, 110, 133; YF 219; BT 102; FTF 21, 38, 105, 161, 184, 187
Cat Legends: LWL 139, 164; FTF 39
Cave: TH 73, 86
Cave of Ancients: CA 79
Chang Tang Highl.: TE 158; DFL 183
Chants: FTF 146
Chakras: WA 24; ChL 181
Characteristics: TC 40
Chariots of Gods: TH 14, 23, 79, 82
Charms: WA 25; BT 115
Children: YF 169; FTF 59, 167, 174, 176; TC 147
Chorten: TE 113
Christianity: ChL 198; BT 27, 102, 107; FTF 135
Civilisations: CA 84; BT 81, 129; YF 153; FTF 147; TH 109, 141, 148
Clairvoyance: TE 78, 151; DFL 117; RS 13; CA 43, 146, 157, YF 147, 160, 168; WA 27; SR 92, 204; ChL 109, 190
Climate: TH 148
Clothing: SR 204; YF 121; TH 56
Collision of Worlds: TH 147
Colours: TH 104, 109, 112
Colours of Aura: CA 212; YF 35, 44; ChL 192
Common Sense: YF 105
Communism: DFL 22; RS 156; ChL 133; BT 108; TH 154
Composure: DFL 206; YF 147, 168
Confession to Maat: ChL 96
Concentration: YF 104; WA 27
Consciousness (1/10): YF 199; BT 121; TC 153-4
Conscious Mind: YF 199
Constantinople Conv.: RS 154; CA 179; YF 119; ChL 214; TH 154
Constipation: SR 180; BT 51
Contamination of Space: TH 91, 123
Controlled Imagination: YF 175, 179
Controlled Thought: TE 87; FTF 144
Control of Organs: ChL 194

159

Crystal Ball: TE 77; DFL 118, 124, 128; SR 144; ChL 109; YF 161
Creation: CA 15; ChL 210
Creation of Universe: TH 123, 134
Cults: WA 28; FTF 48; TC 104
Curses: BT 117

Death: TE 101, 104, 173; DFL 97, 100; RS 76; CA 35; YF 30, 187; WA 29; ChL 120, 128; BT 13, 20, 70; FTF 18, 122; TH 42, 157; TC 14, 22, 28, 123
Developing Occult Abilities: FTF 116
Devils: WA 31; ChL 94; FTF 27; TH 19; TC 31
Dialogue of Plato: ChL 77
Diet: WA 32
Dimensions: WA 33; ChL 33, 41, 63, 67, 69, 75; TH 109
Discipline: YF 197, 215; BT 104
Doctors: BT 70; FTF 160; TC 36
Dogs: RS 49, 51
Doing Good: YF 154; TC 44
Doing Right: BT 98
Dreams: WA 35; YF 118; FTF 72
Drinks: YF 197, 217
Drugs: BT 67; FTF 61; YF 73, 197
Dwarfs: TH 16, 26, 107, 128

Earth: BT 128; FTF 152; TH 135, 139
Earth Cycles: ChL 20
Earth–Life–School: CA 194; YF 92, 114, 126, 144; SR 85; ChL 20; FTF 113, 139; TC 130
Earth Magnetism: BT 118
Earth (Populating): TH 135, 137, 139
Education: FTF 59
Electricity: DFL 49; CA 13, 75, 108, 111; YF 19, 129, 150; ChL 183; FTF 181
Elementals: YF 73; WA 37; ChL 112, 156, 177; FTF 166; TC 17, 31–2
Embalming: TE 178; FTF 65
Emotions: YF 148, 166, 168; WA 38; ChL 110; TC 41
Etheric: YF 25; WA 39; ChL 192; FTF 56
Etheric Energy: YF 107; TC 146
Euthanasia: TC 140, 147
Evolution: WA 39; ChL 114; TH 148; TC 113
Extra-Sensory Power: BT 98
Extra-terrestrials: TH 111
Extremes: ChL 51; FTF 26
Eyes: WA 41

Face: WA 42
Fall of Man: TE 106
Faith: YF 142
Faith Healers: FTF 159
Faults: ChL 204
Fear: CA 39, 136; YF 61, 72, 111, 135; WA 43; ChL 26, 110; BT 97; TC 32, 33, 41
Females: TH 29, 64, 77, 80

Fire: TH 33
Flowers: FTF 152
Flying: DFL 72, 137
Food: CA 217; YF 216; WA 148; FTF 148
Forcing Shed: TH 129
Fortune Tellers: FTF 47
Fourth Dimension. ChL 75

Galaxies: TH 16
Garden of Eden: RS 91; ChL 209
Gardeners of Earth: FTF 148, 150; TH 14, 73, 82, 110, 140, 147, 150, 154; TC 154
Cautama: TH 151; TC 118
Genius Children: FTF 174
Ghosts: DFL 87; CA 21, 28, 216; YF 17, 31, 112; WA 46; FTF 177
Giants: TH 16, 26, 61, 107, 128
Give: YF 97, 171; ChL 198, 200
God: TE 79, 101, 183; CA 60; WA 47; ChL 130; FTF 19, 135, 138; YF 108; TC 100
Gods: TH 149, 150
Gods of the Sky: TH 14
Golden Rule: YF 193; TH 152; TC 118, 128
Graphology: FTF 92
Greed: ChL 205
Guide: FTF 131; TC 19, 100, 103

Harmony: YF 95, 117; TH 152
Healing: WA 53; TC 145, 146
Hearing: TH 70, 74
Hell: CA 54; DFL 102; ChL 94; BT 20; FTF 19, 139, 177; TC 32
Herbs: TE 122, 127; RS 38; DFL 56, 109, 192; SR 159; BT 58, 131, 140
Hermits: TE 87; DFL 112, 183; CA 69; SR 34, 216; TH 7, 69, 71; TC 61
History: TC 141–2
History of Earth: DFL 159; BT 81; TH 110
Holy Eight-Fold Path: SR 71; WA 23
Homosexuality: FTF 98; TC 34; Chapters 3 and 4
Horoscope: TE 110; CA 219; YF 196; ChL 184; FTF 89
Humans: RS 36; CA 215; YF 117; ChL 179; BT 126; FTF 134, 150; TH 127, 146
Humanoids: RS 36; BT 126; TH 61, 85, 107, 112, 120, 128, 140, 146
Hypnotism: TE 167; DFL 93; CA 100, 107, 113; YF 199, 204, 210; WA 55; ChL 110, 157; FTF 58
Hysteria: YF 167; FTF 57
Hysterectomy: BT 62; YF 153

Illness: DFL 204; CA 198; YF 145; BT 68, 131; FTF 130, 163, 181; TH 93, 140; TC 99–100
Illusion: CA 27, 32; WA 57
Imagination: DFL 90; CA 181; YF 121, 175; WA 58
Incarnation: TE 126; YF 94; WA 59; FTF 168
Influencing others: FTF 80, 92
Initiation: TE 188
Inner Composure: YF 147

Insanity: CA 74; FTF 163
Interpenetration: ChL 65
Intuition: YF 156
Invisible Ship: ChL 75
Invisibility: TE 167; ChL 75

Jesus: TH 152
Jews: YF 109; ChL 22
Judo: TE 51, 95; YF 105
Justin (Letter): TC 38

Keep Calm: YF 166, 168
Kharma: RS 118; CA 43; YF 181; WA 63; ChL 187; BT 68; FTF 158, 164, 169, 172; TC 100
Kidneys: BT 140
Kites: TE 18, 128
Kundalini: RS 91 WA 66; ChL 182; FTF 57

Lamaism: TE 115; SR 21
Lamasery: TE 96; SR 18
Land of Golden Light: TE 113; RS 75, 139; ChL 177
Laws: TE 17, 59, 119; SR 87; WA 68; TC 155
Learning: CA 53, 193; BT 100; TC 43–4, 127
Legends: TE 78, 163; BT 120; TH 147, 150
Levitation: TE 168; WA 70; ChL 106
Life: CA 10, 19, 53, 194; YF 13, 92; RS 37
Life before Birth: FTF 68
Life Force: YF 88
Life Forms: RS 35
Light: ChL 209; FTF 185
Light Waves: YF 137
Lincoln–Kennedy: FTF 82
Lost Ships: ChL 55; FTF 148

Magnetism: DFL 60; YF 24; ChL 53; FTF 56
Magnetic Fields: FTF 56; YF 24
Mantras: YF 79, 143; WA 77; FTF 38, 92
Manu: CA 62; WA 78; ChL 113; FTF 37, 135, 138
Marriage: CA 202; YF 116
Master of the World: TH 108, 114, 119
Meat Eating: YF 216
Meditation: WA 79; ChL 129, 142, 149; BT 124, 126; FTF 50, 141
Mediums: WA 80; ChL 104, 112, 114; FTF 14; TC 14, 102
Memory: TE 71; WA 81; FTF 77; TH 23, 77
Menopause: YF 153; BT 60
Mental Control: DFL 206
Mental Illness: FTF 163
Mental Relaxation: TE 118
Metaphysics: FTF 50, 53
Middle Way: TE 119; SR 45, 78; YF 105, 130, 169
Mind Control: DFL 154; SR 77; YF 170
Molecules: YF 13; TH 133
Monk: TE 64; TC 51

Moods: CA 211; YF 125, 127
Moses: BT 66; TH 92, 151
Musik: YF 50

Names: YF 190
Nature Spirits: CA 19; YF 61, 73, 120; WA 86
Neck: WA 86
Negative Feed-back: YF 104
Negative Treatment: ChL 188
Negroes: FTF 157
Nervous Force: DFL 203; FTF 178
Nirvana: SR 78; WA 89; ChL 148
Numerology: WA 90

Obedience: YF 95
Observatory of Worlds: TH 119, 121, 139
Occultism: WA 93; ChL 104; YF 107
Occult Powers: CA 142; WA 93; ChL 105
Occult Proof?: FTF 65
Olympus: TH 149
Opening of Mind: TH 65-6
Opinions: YF 218
Organ Transplant: FTF 142
Origin of Gods: TH 23
Ouija Boards: FTF 132
'Out of this World': YF 113
Overself: CA 33; YF 20, 59; WA 95; ChL 36, 94; FTF 85, 98, 133, 173, 179; TH 117; TC 17, 96, 99, 101, 103, 132, 134

Pain: DFL 154, 207; WA 101; FTF 107, 130; TC 97-8
Palmistry: FTF 94, 176
Paper: SR 119
Parables: RS 23, 197, 219; ChL 70
Parallel Worlds: ChL 33, 95
Parents: YF 95
Parties: YF 88
Planes of Existence: WA 100
Planet Zhoro: RS 32
Plants: FTF 150; TH 135, 139
People: TH 25, 26
Perjury: ChL 205
Petroleum: BT 130
Poems, concealed: ChL 84
Polarity: ChL 45
Police: TC 58, 94, 108
Populating new Earth: TH 135, 137, 139
Power: WA 102
Power of the Mind: TE 170
Prayer: TE 103; RS 142; CA 56; SR 94, 192, 196; WA 104; ChL 98; FTF 58, 144; TH 42; TC 25, 27, 29, 145
Predictions–Probabilities: TE 37, 109, 125; CA 43; ChL 25, 133, 137; BT 143; FTF 85
Press: FTF 42, 63, 92; TC 49, 58, 62, 79-80

Priests: TH 11, 141, 149, 150, 153
Prince Satan: TH 147, 150
Problems: YF 106
Prophecies: CA 206; BT 143
Proof: WA 105; FTF 65; YF 120; TC 13, 16
Psychometry: TE 112; CA 51; YF 147, 156, 162; WA 105; ChL 206;
    BT 99; TH 76
Punctuality: YF 195
Purgatory: TC 110

Race: TH 129
Race of Tan: FTF 153
Race Protectors: TH 148
Radiation: TH 132
Radio: YF 104, 148, 149, 181; TH 119; TC 135
Reason: TH 59
Rebirth: TE 104; CA 35; FTF 68, 81, 127
Record: TH 88
Record of Probabilities: ChL 137; BT 37
Re-creation: YF 129; WA 109
Refuges: SR 80
Re-incarnation: TE 60; WA 109; FTF 35, 81, 127, 170; YF 112; TC
    134, 135-6
Rejoice: YF 107
Relativity: ChL 72
Relaxation: TE 117; YF 84, 206; WA 109; ChL 195
Relaxation Exercises: TC 68, 70, 71
Religion: CA 55, 63, 178, 181; YF 106, 195; SR 189, 196; ChL 214; BT
    108; FTF 28, 154; TH 92, 154; TC 40, 127
Reversed Effort: FTF 51, 57
Right Mindfulness: SR 77
Rules for Right Living: YF 193

Sacrifice: ChL 204
Satan: FTF 27; TH 147, 150
Scandal: ChL 204
Science: TH 47
Scientists: ChL 33, 216; TH 11
School of Life: CA 202; YF 144
Seance: WA 113; FTF 131; TC 14, 17, 101
Sea of Space: TH 79
Seer: YF 115
Sex: CA 173, 178; RS 94; ChL 147; BT 24, 65, 69
Sight: TH 12, 24, 27, 45, 52, 86
Silence: YF 88, 90
Silver Cord: TE 105; RS 31; CA 34; YF 20, 59; WA 116; ChL 122; FTF
    97, 165; TC 99, 103, 132
Sleep: YF 113, 127; FTF 70
Sleep Learning: FTF 75
Socrates: FTF 96
Sodom and Gomorrah: TH 150
Solar System: TH 132
Soul: CA 33; WA 117; TC 14

Soul (Freeing): TE 174; TC 25, 27, 29
Sounds: YF 44; FTF 30, 146; TC 135
Space: TH 88, 121, 124, 133
Space Cities: TH 106, 119, 125
Space Expeditions: TH 132, 137
Space Ships: TH 14, 23, 73, 79, 82, 88, 107, 122, 125, 127, 133, 140
Space Worlds: TH 104, 106, 119, 132
Spirit Guides: FTF 31
Spirits: ChL 113; FTF 177; TH 128
Stars: TH 104, 124
Stones: WA 118, 141
Subconscious: YF 198; ChL 37; BT 121; FTF 77; TC 99
Suffering: SR 60; YF 92, 144, 145, 183, 191; BT 108; TC 112
Suicide: RS 15; CA 38, 205; FTF 63, 128; TC 127, 140, 143
Sun: TH 134

Talisman: BT 115
Tarot: WA 121
Tea: SR 17; TH 101; TC 85
Telepathy: TE 106, 167; RS 191; CA 23, 118; YF 88, 147, 156, 168;
    WA 122; BT 152
Telepathy with Animals: FTF 160; TC 105
Teleportation: WA 122; ChL 69
Telescope: TE 85
Temple Sleep: ChL 158
Think Strength: TH 89
Tibet: RS 17, 154; FTF 41; TH 92
Tibetan Prayer for the Dead: TE 103, 135; SR 94; CA 27; TH 42; TC
    25, 27, 29
Time: ChL 52, 68; FTF 118; TH 139
Time Capsule: CA 85; FTF 146
Time Cycle: TE 108; RS 37; ChL 52, 177; FTF 177
Time Travel: YF 140
Tithe: YF Less. 14; ChL 198, 200
Thought: YF 62, 65, 184, 198; TH 59, 77, 110
Thought, controlled: TE 87; YF 88; FTF 144
Thought Forms: RS 147; CA 66; BT 117
Thought Power: CA 161
Thought Waves: FTF 50
Tolerance: TC 148
Toothache: BT 148
Touchstones: WA 123, 147; BT 115; FTF 29, 141
Trance: YF 210; WA 123; ChL 156
Tranquillity: YF 147, 151
Transmigration: RS 14, 79, 141, 154, 162, 177, 210; YF 184; ChL 23,
    26; FTF 175; TH 153, TC 149
Twin Soul: ChL 186; FTF 173

UFO: TE 104; ChL 54, 211; BT 28, 66, 75, 85; TH 14, 23, 73, 79, 82,
    88, 107, 122, 125, 133 140
Ulcers: YF 152
Unconsciousness: TH 29

Unit of Life: RS 37
Universes: RS 37; CA 10; TH 14, 108, 120, 124, 147

Vegetarianism: YF 217; FTF 148
Vibrations: CA 10, 21, 28, 205, 212; YF 21, 42, 47, 123, 137, 190; ChL
   51; BT 151; FTF 145, 146; TH 76; TC 134-5
Voices: TH 15, 23, 60, 62; TC 81
Voice of Gods: TH 149

War: CA 48, 186; YF 92; FTF 32, 154; TH 147
Waves, elec.: YF 137
Wheel of Existence: TE 66
Wheel of Life: TE 101; YF 183
Willpower: YF 175
Winged Spirits: TH 128
Wise Ones: TH 122, 124, 127, 141, 146, 152
Women: BT 105, 110; YF 13; TC 62, 136-7
Worlds: TH 88, 93, 124, 127, 129
World Leader: ChL 23
World Observ. Apparatus: TH 49, 53
World of Anti-Matter: ChL 54
World of Illusion: CA 32; TH 117
Work: YF 215
Works of Man: ChL 179
Worries: YF 154

Yeti: TE 161
Yoga: TE 168; SR 168; WA 131; YF 196; TC 116

Zagreb Letter: YF 133
Zodiac Signs: ChL 185

More yet—now you get the 'Wise Sayings'
as a bonus, too!

WISE SAYINGS

It is better to light a candle than to curse the darkness — FTF 6

The more you know the more you have to learn. — FTF 9

Never reply to criticism; to do so is to weaken your case. — FTF 26

Everything that exists has motion. — FTF 27

Without extremes how can there be anything? — FTF 27

It is not bad to have extremes, it just means that two points are separated from each other as far as they can be. — FTF 27

The right path is close at hand yet mankind searches for it afar. — FTF 41

Success is the culmination of hard work and thorough preparation. — FTF 56

A hundred men may make a camp; it takes a woman to make a home. — FTF 70

Time is the most valuable thing a man can spend. — FTF 87

Injure others and you injure yourself. — FTF 107

If people would plan their days properly and stick to the plan, there would be adequate time for everything. This is the Voice of Experience because I practise what I teach—successfully! — FTF 119

If you don't scale the mountain you can't view the plain. — FTF 120

Remember, the turtle progresses only when he sticks out his neck. — FTF 138

The gem cannot be polished without friction, nor man perfected without trials. — FTF 155

A man has to hold his mouth open a long time before a roasted partridge flies into it. — FTF 172

If you don't believe in others how can you expect other to believe in you? — FTF 184

Divide the enemy and you can rule the enemy, stay united yourself and you can defeat a divided enemy. The enemy can well be indecision, fear, and uncertainty. — SR 87

Humans—man and woman—must try to live with each other exercising tolerance, patience, and selflessness. ChL 187

By keeping pure thoughts, we keep out unpure thoughts, we strengthen that to which we return when we leave the body. SR 194

One can ask in prayer that one shall be able to assist others, because through assisting others one learns oneself, in teaching others one learns oneself, in saving others one saves oneself. One has to give before one can receive, one has to give of oneself, give of one's compassion, of one's mercy. Until one is able to give of oneself, one is not able to receive from others. One cannot obtain mercy without first showing mercy. One cannot obtain understanding without first having given understanding to the problems of others. SR 196

Return good for evil and fear no man, and fear no man's deed, for in returning good for evil and giving good at all times, we progress upwards and never downwards. YF 22

To the pure, all things are pure. YF 55

Whatever you believe you are, that you are. Whatever you believe you can do, that you can do. YF 77

Be still and know that I am within. YF 90

Give that you may receive. YF 102

What a person fears, that he persecutes. YF 109

We fear that which we do not understand. YF 112

When we are on the other side of death we are living in harmony. YF 117

'Unless you be as little children you cannot enter into the kingdom of heaven' should read:
'If you have the belief of a child uncontaminated by adult disbelief you can go anywhere at any time.' YF 120

Dreams are windows into another world. YF 128

If you keep on telling yourself that you are going to succeed, you will succeed, but you will only succeed if you keep on with your affirmation of success and not let doubt (the negative faith) intrude. YF 144

We must at all times cultivate inner composure, cultivate tranquil manner. YF 150

The distilled essence of all that we learn upon Earth is that which makes us what we are going to be in the next life. YF 150

Ask yourself: will any of these matters, any of these

worries, be important in fifty or a hundred years time? YF 153

The more good you can do to others, the more you gain yourself. YF 154

If you think peace, you will have peace. YF 155

We must be at peace within ourselves if we are going to progress. YF 156

With inner composure and faith you can do ANYTHING. YF 164

As we think today so we are tomorrow. YF 166

If you are showing the effects of strain it means that you do not have the correct perspective. YF 169

If you work too hard you are so busy thinking about the hard work you are putting in that you have no time to think about the results you hope to obtain. YF 169

It is well to remember that in any battle between the imagination and the will power, the imagination always wins. YF 175

If you will cultivate your imagination and control it, you can have whatever you want. YF 179

The only thing to be afraid of is of being afraid. YF 180

If you control your imagination by building up faith in your own abilities, you can do anything. YF 180

There is no such thing as 'impossible'. YF 180

As you think, so you are. YF 184

We should forgive those that trespass against us, and we should seek the forgiveness of those against whom we trespass. We should always remember that the surest way to a good Kharma is to do to others as we would have them do to us. YF 185

In the eye of God all men are equal, and in the eye of God all creatures are equal whether they be horses or cats, etc. YF 185

We should at all times show great care, great concern, great understanding for those who are ill or sorrowing or are afflicted, for it may be that our task is to show such care and understanding. YF 185

The sick person may well be far more evolved than are you who are healthy, and in helping that sick person you could indeed help yourself immensely. YF 186

Sorrowing unduly for those who have 'passed over' causes them pain, causes them to be dragged down to Earth. YF 190

Just as we should do as we would be done by, we should give full tolerance, full freedom to another person to believe and worship as he or she thinks fit. YF 195

Failure means that you were not really strong in your resolution to do this or not do that! YF 213

The beggar of today might be the prince of tomorrow, and the prince of today might be the beggar of tomorrow. YF 216

Do not at any time inflict your own opinion on others. YF 217

Those who talk least hear most. WA 120

The mind is like a sponge which soaks up knowledge. WA 81

Peace is the absence of conflict internally and externally. WA 99

This world, this life, is the testing place wherein our spirit is purified by the suffering of learning to control our gross flesh body. CA 33

There can be an evil man in a Lamasery just as there can be a saint in prison. CA 47

We came to this world to suffer that our Spirit may evolve. Hardship teaches, pain teaches, kindness and consideration do not. CA 62

Fear corrodes the Soul. CA 141

Life follows a hard and stony path, with many traps and pitfalls, yet if one perseveres the top is attained. CA 145

The greatest force in the world is imagination. CA 181

Let your conscience by your guide. CA 188

Never dispair, never give up, for right will prevail. CA 188

You cannot have a cultured man unless that man has been disciplined. CA 196

It is a sad fact that we learn only with pain and suffering. CA 197

There must be love between the parents if the best type of child is to be born. CA 203

Almost any couple could live together successfully provided they learn this matter of give and take. CA 203

Do not quarrel or be at variance with each other, for the child absorbs the attitude of the parents. The child of unkind parents becomes unkind. CA 210

The master always comes when the student is ready. CA 223

Iron ore may think itself senselessly tortured in the furnace, but when the tempered blade of finest steel looks back it knows better. RS 14

He who listens most learns most. RS 96

Race, creed, and colour do not matter, all men bleed red. RS 138

Imagination is the greatest force on Earth. RS 149

It is not good to dwell too much upon the past when the whole future is before one. DFL 43

It is better to rest with a peaceful mind than to sit like a Buddha and pray when angry. TE 58

It is a sad thing that people condemn that which they do not understand. ChL 137

There is a definite occult law which says that you cannot receive unless you are first ready to give. ChL 200

'Let there be light' means 'lift the Soul of man out of darkness that he may perceive the Greatness of God'. ChL 209

Death to Earth is birth into the Astral World. BT 20

All depends upon your attitude, upon your frame of mind, because as we think so we are. BT 64

This Earth is just a speck of dust existing for the twinkle of an eye in what is real time. FTF 24

Everyone HAS to be an island unto himself. FTF 48

Suicide is never justified. FTF 64

Your body is just a vehicle, a vehicle whereby your Overself can gain some experience on Earth. FTF 76

Man, when evolved, can have his 'service' within himself, anywhere, at any time, without having to be herded and congregated like mindless yaks. TH 10

The more a man's spirituality the less his worldy possessions. TH 11

One without eyes is particularly helpless, completely at the mercy of others, at the mercy of EVERYTHING. TH 15

Man is temporary, man is frail, life on Earth is but illusion and the Greater Reality lies beyond. TH 43

Appearances can be misleading. TH 48

Rumours are never reliable. TH 91

Some of us are doing our best in very difficult circumstances and our hardships were to encourage us to do better and climb upwards, for there is always room at the top! TH 98

THIS is the shadow life. If we do our task in THIS life we shall go to the REAL life hereafter. I know that for I have seen it. TH 103

Time upon Earth is just a flickering in the consciousness of cosmic time. TH 108

Learn to endure hunger now. Learn fortitude now. Learn always to have a positive approach NOW, for during your life you will know hunger and suffering; they will be your constant companions. There are many who will harm you, many who will attempt to drag you down to their level. Only by a positive mind—always positive—will you survive and surmount all these trials and tribulations which inexorably will be yours. Now is the time to learn. ALWAYS is the time to practice what you learn now. So long as you have faith, so long as you are POSITIVE, then you can endure the worst assaults of the enemy. TH 117

No man is given more than he can bear, and man himself chooses what tasks he shall perform, what tasks he shall undergo. TH 117

One of the main troubles of this world is that most people are negative. TH 155

If people would always think POSITIVELY there would be no trouble with the world, for the negative condition comes naturally to people here, although it actually takes more effort to be negative. TH 156

Man upon Earth is an irrational figure given to believing that which is not so in preference to that which is. TC 33

You may get a very good person who gets a lot of pain and you—the onlooker—may think it is unfair that such a person should have such suffering, or you may think that the person concerned is paying back an exceedingly hard Kharma. But you could be wrong. How do you know that the person is not enduring the pain and suffering in order to see how pain and suffering can be eliminated for those who come after? Do not think that it is always paying back Kharma. It may possibly be accumulating good Kharma. TC 104

We have to manage on our own, everyone of us. It is wrong to join cults and groups. We have to stand alone, and if Man is to evolve Man must be alone. TC 108

This is the Age of Kali, the Age of Disruption, the Age of Change when mankind stands at the crossroads deciding to evolve or devolve, deciding whether to go upwards or whether to sink down to the level of the chimpanzee. And in this, the Age of Kali, I have come in an attempt to give some knowledge and perhaps to weigh a decision to Western man and woman that it is better to study and climb upwards than to sit still and sink down into the slough of despond. TC 112

You can be reaching for Buddhahood whatever your station in life. The only thing to go on is—how

172

do you live? Do you live according to the Middle Way, do you live according to the rule that you should do as you would have others do unto you? If so, then you are on the road to Buddhahood. TC 118

We came to this Earth for the purpose of developing our Immortal Soul. TC 127

We come to this Earth knowing before we come what our problem will be, knowing what hardships we shall have to undergo, and if we commit suicide then we are running out on arrangements which we ourselves made for our own advancement. TC 128

Anything you do here benefits your Overself and so benefits you because you are the same thing. TC 133

Without the Press causing race hatred there would not be so much trouble between the different colours of humans. TC 139

If you are afraid you are dissipating your energy needlessly. TC 153

DO AS YOU WOULD HAVE OTHERS DO
UNTO YOU

THREE LIVES
By T. LOBSANG RAMPA

This book continues the theme of Dr Rampa's previous book I BELIEVE in that it is a further statement of his personal belief in life after death, and his thoughts on the nature of the afterlife. Free from prejudice, free from the dogmas of organised religion, Dr Rampa's beliefs have been formed by years of study, years of offering comfort and inspiration to his countless followers all over the world.

THREE LIVES will be welcomed by the many thousands of readers who turn to Dr Rampa for consolation and guidance.

0 552 10707 7—75p

AS IT WAS!
By T. LOBSANG RAMPA

The Chief Astrologer of Tibet had been summoned to proclaim the horoscope of the six-year-old Lobsang, son of Lord and Lady Rampa. It was the most difficult reading, the hardest life he had ever encountered, the old man said. The boy was going to learn all the medical arts of Tibet, and then journey to China to study medicine in the Western style. He would know immense suffering and dreadful hardship, travel in many countries, be unjustly imprisoned. But above all, the boy's lonely destiny would be to carry out a great task of the utmost importance to all humanity – and evil forces would work against him to thwart his efforts . . .

AS IT WAS! is a fascinating account of the life and achievements of a remarkable man.

0 552 10087 0—£1.00

A SELECTED LIST OF PSYCHIC, MYSTIC AND OCCULT TITLES FROM CORGI

WHILE EVERY EFFORT IS MADE TO KEEP PRICES LOW, IT IS SOMETIMES NECESSARY TO INCREASE PRICES AT SHORT NOTICE. CORGI BOOKS RESERVE THE RIGHT TO SHOW AND CHARGE NEW RETAIL PRICES ON COVERS WHICH MAY DIFFER FROM THOSE ADVERTISED IN THE TEXT OR ELSEWHERE.

THE PRICES SHOWN BELOW WERE CORRECT AT THE TIME OF GOING TO PRESS (DECEMBER '80).

☐ 09828 0	THE PROPHECIES OF NOSTRADAMUS	Erika Cheetham	£1.50
☐ 08800 5	CHARIOTS OF THE GODS?	Erich Von Daniken	£1.25
☐ 09083 2	RETURN TO THE STARS	Erich Von Daniken	95p
☐ 09689 X	THE GOLD OF THE GODS	Erich Von Daniken	£1.25
☐ 10073 0	IN SEARCH OF ANCIENT GODS	Erich Von Daniken	85p
☐ 10371 3	MIRACLES OF THE GODS	Erich Von Daniken	85p
☐ 10870 7	ACCORDING TO THE EVIDENCE	Erich Von Daniken	£1.25
☐ 11020 5	THE GHOST OF FLIGHT 401	John G. Fuller	£1.25
☐ 11220 8	MY SEARCH FOR THE GHOST OF FLIGHT 401	Elizabeth Fuller	£1.00
☐ 09430 7	THE U.F.O. EXPERIENCE – A SCIENTIFIC INQUIRY	John Allen Hynek	95p
☐ 10928 2	THE ANCIENT MAGIC OF THE PYRAMIDS	Ken Johnson	80p
☐ 14609 2	LIFE AFTER LIFE	Raymond A. Moody Jr. M.D.	£1.00
☐ 11140 X	REFLECTIONS ON LIFE AFTER LIFE	Raymond A. Moody Jr. M.D.	£1.00
☐ 10707 7	THREE LIVES	T. Lobsang Rampa	75p
☐ 10628 3	DOCTOR FROM LHASA	T. Lobsang Rampa	£1.25
☐ 11464 2	THE CAVE OF THE ANCIENTS	T. Lobsang Rampa	£1.00
☐ 10416 7	I BELIEVE	T. Lobsang Rampa	75p
☐ 10189 3	THE SAFFRON ROBE	T. Lobsang Rampa	£1.25
☐ 10087 0	AS IT WAS!	T. Lobsang Rampa	£1.00
☐ 09834 5	THE THIRD EYE	T. Lobsang Rampa	£1.00
☐ 11413 8	THE RAMPA STORY	T. Lobsang Rampa	95p
☐ 11283 6	AUTUMN LADY	Mama San Ra-Ab Rampa	85p
☐ 11315 8	GHOSTS OF WALES	Peter Underwood	£1.25

All these books are available at your bookshop or newsagent; or can be ordered direct from the publisher. Just tick the titles you want and fill in the form below.

CORGI BOOKS, Cash Sales Department, P.O. Box 11, Falmouth, Cornwall.

Please send cheque or postal order, no currency.

U.K. Please allow 30p for the first book, 15p for the second book and 12p for each additional book ordered to a maximum charge of £1.29.

B.F.P.O. and Eire allow 30p for the first book, 15p for the second book plus 12p per copy for the next 7 books, thereafter 6p per book.

Overseas customers. Please allow 50p for the first book plus 15p per copy for each additional book.

NAME (block letters) ....

ADDRESS ....

(DEC. 1980) ....